Creating Your Career:

Mastering the Changing Nature of Work

Denise O'Brien

Manor House

Creating Your Career / Denise O'Brien

Library and Archives Canada Cataloguing in Publication

Title: Creating your career : mastering the changing nature of work / Denise O'Brien.

Names: O'Brien, Denise, 1960- author.

Identifiers: Canadiana 20200341294 |

ISBN 9781988058597 (hardcover) |

ISBN 9781988058580 (softcover)

Subjects: LCSH: Vocational guidance. |
LCSH: Career development.
Classification: LCC HF5381 .O27 2020 |
DDC 650.14—dc23

Cover art: Hermann Eske / Shutterstock

First Edition
Cover Design-layout / Interior- layout: Michael Davie
Edited by Susan Crossman, Crossman Communications
236 pages / 48,879 words. All rights reserved.

Published Oct. 15, 2020 / Copyright 2020
Manor House Publishing Inc.
452 Cottingham Crescent, Ancaster, ON, L9G 3V6
www.manor-house-publishing.com (905) 648-4797

Funded by the Government of Canada |

Creating Your Career / Denise O'Brien

This book is dedicated to my Grandmother, Mary Denise Molloy, the strongest, most determined, thoughtful, and deeply appreciative woman I've ever known.

Creating Your Career / Denise O'Brien

Acknowledgements

To the many, many people in my life who generously and graciously shared their time and experiences with me as I was researching and writing this book, I send, from the bottom of my heart, a very big "Thank you." The list is long and I hope I don't leave anyone out because each person contributed perspectives that helped illuminate my thoughts.

Thank you to Mark, Susan, Carmel, Carol, Carmen, Marion, Sarah, Chantal, Cecilia, Lee, Susan, Elaine, Benoit, Jackie, Brenda, Cindy, Kelly, Meena, Lucy, Elfie, Tim, Cindy S., Andrea, Lee-Anne, Heather, Janice, Meghan and Lorraine for your amazing support. Thanks also to Manor House for publishing my book.

The opportunity to write this book is just another example of the way in which I have been truly blessed in my life with much love and support.

Malcolm Gladwell[1] (2008) proposed in his book *Outliers* that one's success is in many ways a reflection of other aspects of life, including our birth family, our birthplace, our birth date, and even the era into which we were born. He surmised that we are successful not only because of our individual exertions, but also as a result of the work and efforts of those who went before us, and those who accompanied us throughout our journey. I wholeheartedly concur. I also want to acknowledge my parents, Frank and Helen O'Brien. As a child I would often say "I can't," to which my father would respond "There is no such word as *can't*." In other words "Yes, you can." I am grateful they instilled in me a "can do attitude."

Finally, thank you to my husband, Warren — a wonderful, patient individual who quietly and in very unassuming ways supports everything I undertake. Warren, thank you for your ongoing support and patience.

---

[1] Malcolm Gladwell, *Outliers: The Story of Success* (New York: Hachette Book Group, 2008)

Creating Your Career / Denise O'Brien

Creating Your Career / Denise O'Brien

Table of Contents

About the Author   9

About this Book   11

Praise for Creating Your Career: 13

Introduction   15

Chapter 1   Getting Started   23

Chapter 2   The Changing Nature of Work   45
                 and Workplaces

Chapter 3   The Growth and Maintenance Phase   85

Chapter 4   Complacency   111

Chapter 5   Women   135

Chapter 6   Plateauing in Our Careers   161

Chapter 7   The Exit Phase   185

Chapter 8   Retirement   211

Final Thoughts   231

Creating Your Career / Denise O'Brien

About the author

Denise O'Brien, PhD, has completed post graduate studies in Adult Education, M.A. (Ed), and Industrial-Organizational Psychology, PhD.

She holds the designation of Qualified Mediator (Q.Med), is an Adler Trained Coach (ACC) and was among the first to attain a Queen's University Masters Certificate in Organization Effectiveness.

With a career that has spanned more than 30 years, O'Brien has investigated, assessed, diagnosed, designed and facilitated workplace interventions for 1000's of teams, individuals and management teams.

An expert mediator, she is highly skilled at helping those in conflict achieve 'win-win' outcomes.

O'Brien, an avid outdoors person, enjoys long walks with her canine companions along the beautiful shores of Lake Ontario.

Creating Your Career / Denise O'Brien

About this book

Creating Your Career is an easy-to-read summary of the best pieces of advice you will ever receive about work.

Since we spend almost 1/3 of our adult life at work, learning how to navigate it more easily and with greater levels of satisfaction is time well-spent.

This book is packed with stories and advice that the author has gathered over many years and from thousands of conversations with others, at different stages in their work-life journey.

Regardless of where you are in your work-life journey, this book has something to offer.

And, the good news is, that wherever you are is exactly where you were meant to be. Don't worry. You'll figure it out, utilizing the advice and insight contained in this book.

Praise for Creating Your Career:

"In unprecedented times, Denise's practical advice and guidance about how to navigate our careers in the current talent shortage is both timely and necessary. Few books are of equal value to the individual contributor and those they report to, but this book most certainly is. If you are serious about battling the engagement epidemic to ensure you are satisfied in your career and those in your organization, this book will direct, inspire and motivate you."

- **Sarah McVanel**, MSc, PCC, CHRL, CSP, CSODP, Chief Recognition Officer, **Greatness Magnified**

"When I was a kid, my dad, a Canadian Armed Forces officer told me: "find a good rut and get comfortable; you're in it a long time." But when he was in his forties he became a commercial pilot, illustrating how dated that thinking was. Mine comes from experience too: write your plans in pencil, your legacy in ink. As we've learned through COVID, there are no guarantees; flight plans are merely a suggestion. It's how we choose to prepare for – and then alter – our journey that determines whether we soar or are in a continuous state of waiting to take off. Informative, relatable and a handy guide for the present and the future, **Creating Your Career - Mastering the Changing Nature of Work** *will open your eyes to the opportunities and horizons that lie before you."*

- **Erin Davis**, Inspirational Keynote Speaker, Best-selling Author, Professional MC, Writer, Broadcaster, Blogger

More Praise for Creating Your Career:

"This insightful and practical book is essential reading for professionals in these turbulent times. Dr. O'Brien shows you how to turbocharge your career by asking yourself the questions that will make the most difference wherever you are in your own world of work."

- **Marilee Adams**, Ph.D. bestselling author of *Change Your Questions, Change Your Life: 12 Powerful Tools for Leadership, Coaching, and Life*

I loved the book! The personal stories, real life stats and the different and varying perspectives interviewers shared are a realistic and practical view of careers and life. This is a must read for everyone, regardless of where they are on their work-life journey.

- **Carmel Perry**, Coach

Creating Your Career / Denise O'Brien

Introduction

Many years of experience as a Human Resources (HR) professional taught me that some job functions within an HR Department — such as recruitment-selection, compensation, benefits, and labour relations — tend to be more highly valued than others.

Although I worked diligently in each of these areas, I was also drawn to other areas of specialty, such as organizational effectiveness, and learning and development.

My work in these areas gave me the opportunity to focus on succession planning, performance management, employee engagement, mentoring, and, in a very miniscule way, I was able to dabble in the area of career development.

I would have loved to have made this an area of greater focus. However, compensation and labour relations tend to be the "meat and potatoes" of human resources, and programs such as learning and development— including career growth and development—tend to drop off an organization's priority list once the employee onboarding process is complete.

This tendency to de-emphasize learning and development programs is further heightened during times of economic downturn. For example, I am writing this book in the midst of the Coronavirus pandemic (COVID-19) and I have heard from colleagues that many organizations have eliminated learning and development budgets as they struggle to stay afloat financially.

In fact, at the point of this writing we have no idea how Covid-19 is going to impact the world of work going forward and many people are undoubtedly going to be in for a bumpy and painful transition to a "new normal" way of working.

We will get through Covid-19 the same way people around the world have been dealing with economic and social upheaval for generations: one uncertain step at a time.

While the future reveals itself to us, I will be earnestly wishing people well in their journey to the next stage of their working life. I have always enjoyed conversations with people about their careers.

In fact, I was so drawn to the topic that I chose to study women in the workplace—and the phenomenon of the "glass ceiling"—for my final research paper during my graduate studies in psychology.

I have devoted a chapter in this book to the topic of women to share some of the findings from my research, and to provide an update on the ways in which women have made, and continue to make, great strides forward.

This subject has been controversial, at times, and there are some who feel the topic is getting old. Aren't we beyond all that now? I invite you to read the chapter and see what you think.

Although progress can be attributed to many factors, I certainly feel the #MeToo movement against the sexual harassment and sexual assault of women in recent years has highlighted the need for attitudes to shift and changes to be made, in the workplace and elsewhere.

Life and Work Experiences

Writing a book about careers has been on my bucket list for a long time. This book is intended to be a practical tool to help inform individuals at any point in their career journey.

In writing this book, I have drawn on experiences from my life and work and I have also invested a significant amount of time conducting qualitative research interviewing people on the front line of their careers, at a variety of different stages.

I'm deeply grateful for the invaluable information I gathered about their experiences and insights, much of which has been heavily integrated into this book. Rest assured that I've used fictitious names throughout!

I have come to understand that at the outset of our work life or career it is wise to avoid anticipating it as the result of a single choice, or the pursuit of a specific path.

Rather, our work life or career is likely to be a meandering journey with no absolute destination in mind. It does, however, unfold in specific phases, all of which are explained in a plethora of books and resources on the topic.

The Phases of a Career

My own experience has shown me that careers happen in three main phases, which I characterize as the Getting Started, Maintenance and Exit phases.

We'll now take a closer look at the crucial Getting Started phase.

Getting Started:

In this phase we are thinking about, and asking, a number of questions, including:

What should I do?

What jobs will be available when I graduate?

How much money will I make?

Will I be able to support myself?

What will my parents think?

What are my friends going to be doing?

Where are my friends going to school?

In this phase it feels as though there are many questions but very few answers. Most elements of a career path seem unknown and, depending on who we ask, we tend to receive almost contradictory information about them.

Over the years I have heard countless stories about the confusion, frustration, and worry individuals experience at this point in their careers, and this is particularly true today, when there is so little certainty about the economy at both a global and a local level.

Not to worry! If you are feeling confused or frustrated, this book might not have all the answers but it does offer sage advice from others who have successfully navigated their careers through other unpredictable times, despite having experienced similar feelings and setbacks.

What you can expect to discover in these pages:

Chapter 1 introduces the terms Work, Career and Job and it outlines the ways in which these terms have quite different meanings, even though they are often used interchangeably. One of the foremost pieces of advice offered by experts to help us find our best career fit is this: we must first know ourselves.

While I fully concur with this advice in principle I believe that as we age and gain life experience we inevitably enjoy various levels of personal growth and development. As a teenager finishing secondary school I was tasked with selecting courses to study in university and I really had no idea what I wanted to choose.

I struggled.

At the time I thought I must be the only person in the world who had no idea what I wanted to do when I grew up. With age and maturity comes wisdom and over the years I have come to realize that many of us struggled as we finished secondary school and had to answer the difficult question of "What's next for me?"

In reality, we learn things about ourselves over time that at a younger age we either could not grasp or were unwilling to see or hear. Growing into ourselves is a byproduct of maturity and life and work experience. This chapter includes insights and perspectives to help inform your choices, whether your goal is to obtain a job, some work, or a career. Navigating the work-life journey is easier when we are clear about our goal.

Chapter 2 explores the changing nature of work and workplaces. No matter where you are on your career path, this chapter will provide an overview of the changing nature of workplaces. It includes a brief introduction to the new "psychological contract" between employees and employers.

For the most part, the days are long gone when we might expect to have a "job for life," with security and steady upward advancement within one organization almost guaranteed. This chapter provides expert insight to help answer the question, "Which jobs will be impacted the most by automation?" As we consider the changing nature of work it is helpful to understand the skills and competencies that will likely be in demand in the coming years.

After selecting the work we will do—and staying at it for a period of time—we typically move into the second phase of our career, which is the Maintenance phase.

Chapter 3 describes the growth and maintenance elements of this phase, including the importance of emotional intelligence and the way in which our emotions can de-rail us at work.

Another important consideration in this phase of our work life is learning how to navigate effective workplace relationships. In this chapter I explore five important relationships: the relationship with your boss, your co-worker and peer relationships, your relationship with the organization, your professional networking relationships, and your personal relationships, as well.

In Chapter 4, I embark upon a discussion of an important aspect of working life, which is not talked about as openly as would be useful and that is complacency. I liken career complacency to mediocrity, passivity, disengagement, entitlement and perhaps even victimhood.

Chapter 5 is dedicated to Women and the ways in which we often navigate our careers. The backdrop for this chapter is a field study I undertook a few years ago to explore the existence of the "glass ceiling." Is it real or imagined?

In Chapter 6, I describe what happens when we arrive at a Career Plateau. I believe it is critical that everyone become familiar with career plateaus because:

a. It is inevitable that at some point we will all arrive at a plateau on the work-life journey.

b. We are likely to achieve many plateaus during the course of our working lives.

c. Achieving a plateau is likely to feel and look like the opposite of an achievement because it tends to be a time of confusion, frustration and fear.

d. Plateaus are a signal that it is time to re-visit our work-life journey and assess other opportunities, while asking ourselves, "Is it time to leave?"

In Section Three of the book, I move us into the last phase of work-life which is the Exit Phase. Beginning with **Chapter 7**, I describe job loss in its many forms—both voluntary and involuntary—as a result of downsizing, restructuring, mergers, bankruptcies and other reasons. I also outline the psychological consequences of job loss.

Although losing employment is unlikely to feel good it does not have to be a negative experience. Rather, it can be a time of opportunity and growth. In this chapter I draw on the life know-how of others who have lost jobs over the course of their careers and the ways in which they changed those experiences into fortuitous opportunities that served to launch them into their next success…and on into even greater levels of satisfaction.

After being in the workplace for many years, there will come a point where one needs to, or at least *should,* consider the possibility of Retirement, and that's the topic of **Chapter 8.** I believe we must know when "to hold 'em, fold 'em, walk away or run" in our careers and in my experience many of us either ignore or misread the cues at this phase in our working lives.

The consequences of either ignoring or misreading the cues are explored later in this book. Again, drawing on the experiences of those who generously shared their stories while I was researching this book, I offer sagacious advice to help navigate the exit and/or retirement phase of one's career.

It has been a joy to write this book and a profoundly interesting experience. My favourite aspect of bringing this book together has related to the many conversations I have enjoyed with amazing and generous individuals.

As you read about their experiences, I hope you will be able to relate to them, see yourself reflected in their stories, and feel inspired, hopeful, and optimistic about your own. Finally, my primary objective in writing this book is to provide practical advice about the work-life journey.

I hope you take away some basic truths, including the idea that whatever point you are at on your work-life journey is exactly where you are meant to be. Don't worry. You'll figure it out.

- Denise O'Brien, Cobourg, Ontario

Chapter 1
Getting Started

No one can go back and make a brand-new start, my friend; but anyone can start from here and make a brand-new end.

—Dan Zadra

Congratulations! If you are reading this book you're likely at a point in life where you are considering options for your career journey. Maybe you are already working in a job you no longer love or feel passionate about. Perhaps you are enjoying your work but aren't feeling particularly content in your current organization. Whatever is inspiring you to read this book, you've already made progress because you are open to considering options. Good for you!

Most of the career-related books I've read start with information about the importance of self-awareness. The authors typically tell readers to begin their career selection process by focusing on learning about themselves so they have a detailed understanding of their personal interests, goals, values, skills, knowledge, education, etc.

While I wholeheartedly agree self-awareness is a significant asset, and very important in being able to make an informed, wise choice about one's career, I do not hold to the belief that it is imperative to know yourself before making a choice.

Rather, start from wherever you are and with whatever knowledge you have about yourself. You'll figure things out as you go along. You'll be fine.

The best teacher in life is experience. Age, experience, and an open mind bring wisdom.

As mentioned previously, much of the information and ideas contained in this book come from the first-hand experiences of the many individuals who generously shared their insights with me. They offered their stories so others might benefit from their experiences – successes as well as setbacks.

Let's begin by clarifying some terminology: Work, Career, and Job.

Work is...

I believe work is a fundamental aspect of life. It involves exerting energy to get things done. The energy we expend takes the form of cognitive and physical effort. Work can be something we're paid to perform, or not.

Work provides us with a purpose. It might not be our sole purpose for living, but certainly work is one component of figuring out what we are meant to be doing in the world.

Work provides structure in our lives, which is essential to all human beings. For example, if I work as a stay-at-home mom, my work is structured around caring for my children and all that entails.

This work also provides me with a purpose that feeds my soul. Those without some form of work often feel at a loss to know their purpose.

Interwoven with the language of work are the terms "career" and "job." I often hear these terms used interchangeably but they really mean quite different things.

Over the course of my research I asked people for their definitions of the terms "career" and "job." Here are some of the insights people shared with me

A Career Is...

- **A collection of experiences.**

    One individual defined career as "a collective of experiences and a journey that brings you to a position where you feel like you're actually contributing your expertise and making an impact in an organization; or it doesn't have to be an organization, just in general utilizing your expertise."

- **A winding road.**

- **A jungle gym rather than a ladder.**

    "I don't think it's the same as it used to be because when I was growing up, I had a vision that (a career) was the journey through life, through your working years. It was structure. It was hierarchy. It was a ladder. You paid your dues."

    "I encompass all of the typical stereotypes of the Baby Boom generation. I think what I found as I moved on was that I could actually create my career to align with my life, and it was more of a jungle gym than a ladder."

- **Something that embodies passion.**

    "I think the biggest difference for me personally is that I'm passionate about my career. Like I wake up excited and with a passion that I can feel inside of me for challenge, excitement, and the people I'm going to meet in my day."

- **Wrapped up with feelings of growth and achievement.**

    "I guess it's the fulfillment of goals and objectives throughout your working life. So, for me it's very much about progression in a particular field where you are satisfied you're making progress and you're continuing to grow."

    "When I graduated from college, I knew I wanted a career. I wanted to start somewhere and progress…through increasing responsibility, increasing leadership and increasing satisfaction with the things that I did. It is the accumulation of different roles that constitutes a career."

- **"It's what you are here to contribute to the world."**

- **"I think career is certainly what you do for a living, (and) how you use your skills and talents to make a difference.** And, ideally it's something that you can find both mission and margin in; purpose and profit."

- **"I think it's the way you make your money and your living but also, it's kind of your identity.** It can be something you're passionate about and the way you make your mark on the world."

- **It brings feelings of joy.**

Creating Your Career / Denise O'Brien

- "For me, career has a lot to do with joy and ease and making a difference."

- "It's your soul's calling. It's your purpose here on this planet."

- "Career is a calling. It something I discovered I can do and felt like I had to do it."

- **A career is aspirational.**

    "It is something you pursue because you love it and you're good at it. Or, maybe you're not really good at it but you apply yourself because you're passionate about it."

A Job Is...

- **One of a series of stepping-stones**

    "I think a job would be experiences and stepping-stones. Each of them is a learning experience where you continue to grow and learn more about yourself and how you can contribute and make value in the business world."

- **A means to an end**

    "A job is something that I would look at as a means to an end. We do it because we have to, whether that's to pay the bills or to get extra money. [It's] something to do. Maybe we fell into it and got too old to change and felt like [we had] to stay. Maybe the job offers security like a defined pension plan so [we] stick it out because [we're] afraid to leave."

- **Boredom**

    "Job sounds boring. It's like your heart is not in it. You're just doing it. It lacks life, I think."

- **Transactional**

    "A job is something that you do transactionally for a rate or a fee or a wage. It's about tasks."

- **Coercion, Duty, Responsibility**

    "If you have a job that means something you're forced to do...I see job as duty and responsibility... A job does not fulfill you, versus a career which may bring fulfillment in and of itself."

- **Not your great work!**

    "A job is something that you're employed to do. You are getting paid for it. It's work but it may not be your great work. When you're lucky enough to be employed in your career, then it's work that you're fortunate to be paid to do. It's great work! It's fun work!"

Thus, the terms career and job resonate quite differently with people. Those with whom I spoke perceive their career as something about which they are passionate. It is aspirational.

It isn't a straight path but rather a "jungle gym" or a "winding road." For some, their career is "the reason they were put on this planet."

On the other hand, the definitions of "job" were quite uninspiring. Terms such as "a means-to-an-end" and "transactional" do not infuse anyone's heart with energy, passion, or purpose. A job is about getting something done to receive a wage; it's about "duty" and "responsibility."

Exercise:

Wherever you are in your journey, I invite you to reflect on the following questions.

- If you are starting out, do you want a career or a job?
- If you are currently working, are you working in a career, or are you in a job?
- Does your work inspire you? Does your work feed your soul and give you purpose?
- Do you regard your work as merely fulfilling your duty and responsibility?
- Do you feel boredom or passion with the work you perform?
- Is your work a stepping-stone towards a specific goal?

Knowing whether you are seeking a career or a job is an important consideration regardless of the point you are at along the work journey.

As one individual shared with me, "I worked in one job pre-college (where) I was a cashier at a grocery store. It was one of the best jobs I've ever had. I had a ton of fun and I made some great friends; in fact, I made my best friend in life there and I knew it was a job. It was a means to an end for me, because I was only doing it to make money to go to college."

The point is, jobs do have a purpose, although it might not be your life's purpose. Be aware of the distinction. It will come in handy throughout your working life.

Choosing a Career

During much of my young life, as I finished secondary school and entered university, I gave considerable thought to the question, "What will I do when I grow up?" Entering university, I felt as though I was likely the only person who lacked the answer to this question. At that juncture in school and life, there was a lot of pressure to select courses because it is said to determine the rest of your life, or at least the career you end up with. Apparently, that has not changed.

Looking back, with the benefit of age and experience, and the insight of others, I realize most of my beliefs and doubts were completely without substance. Yes, it is helpful to start and complete post-secondary education with a clear career goal in mind. However, the reality is that most of us who eventually settle into work about which we're passionate and inspired, did not have the capacity or foresight to know this when we started out.

Don't worry. You'll figure it out. Whatever choice you make, opportunities will present for learning at many points along your journey. Seize those opportunities!

"I Knew From Childhood What I Would Do"

I've had many conversations with individuals about how they ended up choosing their respective career paths. It is rare for someone to tell me they knew what they wanted to do, and were meant to be doing, even as children. In those rare situations when I hear for example, "I knew at 13-years of age my career path would be …" These remarks are often followed by comments such as …

> *"I had a teacher who helped me see I had a gift in this area."*

"My father was an accountant and I was always good at math. I thought accounting was what I was supposed to be doing."

"I always loved helping, even as a child, and nursing is a perfect fit. I love it."

"My family is in the car business; I kinda fell into it."

In other words, some of you may have known at any early age what you were "put on this planet to do." But most of us find our way through trial and error and doubt. I hope this book and the collection of wisdom shared by others will alleviate the doubt you may be feeling. You are right where you were meant to be in your life's work. Don't worry. You'll figure it out.

Finding Your Life's Work

I know you'll figure it out because most of us have been at the same point in our lives, trying to figure out the best way forward – and we made it! You'll figure it out, too. However, to reassure you that others have struggled, here are some examples of the fortuitous approaches that have influenced the career paths of others.

1. Career choice often occurs by happenstance

Believe it or not, serendipity and chance are often the main influences of how many people end up in their respective work and career path. Here's how "Janice" chose her career:

"I applied for a government-sponsored program, and I qualified to learn shorthand and typing. I then looked around Sheridan Park in Oakville, Ontario, and I liked the look of the buildings, so I decided I wanted to work in one of them. They were all modern buildings.

I didn't care which building I worked in. I just threw my résumé in at every front desk.

"And then I got a call from a pharmaceutical firm, so I went there. I had no idea what they did. It was during the days [when] you didn't research that sort of thing. I just knew they had an opening for somebody with my secretarial skills."

Another woman, "Shelly" explained her experience this way:

"When I graduated from university it was in the middle of a recession and jobs were scarce. I had graduated with a degree in social sciences and I had no idea what I was going to be able to do with it. I did a few temporary jobs in businesses that had nothing to do with what I'd studied.

"However, I thought that a government agency might hire someone with a university degree, so I kept applying for anything and everything. Eventually, I got an interview. I ended up staying."

Both women shared how they began their career "quite by chance" and their careers worked out perfectly fine. I could share many, many examples of the happenstance way in which most of us approach our work and career choices but I think you get the point.

Many years ago, I read an article which pointed out that most of us expend greater time researching, reflecting, stressing over, selecting, and ultimately choosing the vehicles we purchase, the first home we buy, and the partner we marry, than we expend in coming to a decision about our life's work and career. In other words, most of us give more thought to our house purchases than we do to figuring out what we want our life's work to be.

How do we want to contribute to the world? What are we passionate about? These are less-pressing issues for most of us.

2. Career choice can be a result of course choices at school

Another way our work and career choices are influenced relates to the courses we choose to complete.

For example, one woman explained that in figuring out her post-secondary path she asked herself "what can I study that I could do for the rest of my life that wouldn't kill me? I literally said those words, "what wouldn't kill me?"

During my many conversations, I heard from some people that they began post-secondary studies with goals in mind around where they might end up in their work. However, along the way their goals and visions changed.

"John" described his experience this way: "I had actually been working in construction right out of high school. I thought I'd go to college and take up a trade. It seemed to be a good fit. Then I kinda got just fascinated with getting into social work."

"Matt" articulated it this way: "At university I studied finance and accounting and thought that was my career path. While studying I got some jobs doing outdoor guiding and teaching and realized I had much more passion and interest and even skill in that area than in accounting."

For this individual, studying in one field but feeling passionate about another area of study influenced him to choose a different career path.

3. Mentors, teachers. and parents influence choices

Research suggests our work and career paths are profoundly influenced by our parents and other adults such as teachers, grandparents, and anyone else who plays a significant role in our young lives. For example, one woman explained that while she was growing up her parents were self-employed entrepreneurs. She was always very aware of the cyclical nature in the demand for her parent's products and services.

And she was sensitive to the financial strains her parents often felt at times when business was slow.

Her parents' experience as entrepreneurs influenced her to seek stability and security through a regular 9-to-5 job. She didn't ask herself "is this what I was meant to be doing on this planet?" Rather, a secure job provided her with a regular pay cheque, which met her needs.

One woman, let's call her Leah, had the wisdom to recognize what she characterized as "programming." Leah recalls that as she entered her teen years many of her friends were planning to head off to college or university. It was expected, and she felt some degree of pressure to conform and follow a similar path of post-secondary education. Although she was grateful to attend university because it opened her mind to new opportunities and ways of thinking,

Creating Your Career / Denise O'Brien

Leah came to realize the path she was following was not right for her. "I believe that every single person has a calling from their soul, but they may have programming that is really, really strong that relates to survival, following others, and following the "right" thing to do instead of *your* thing to do."

Of course, I'm sure Leah's parents wanted only the best for her by encouraging her or perhaps coercing Leah to attend post-secondary education. They might have been fearful that if she didn't attend college or university, she would not be able to support herself and life would undoubtedly hold more struggles.

A wonderful book by Dr. Susan Jeffers, *Feel the Fear and Do it Anyway*[2] points out that parents often instill fear in their children without meaning to do so.

For example, Dr. Jeffers wisely asks, "Do you ever recall a time in your life when your parents said to you, "Go out and take some risks today!"? Of course not! Parents want to keep their children safe. Parents tend to want their children to enjoy lives that are free from too many struggles.

Keeping our children safe often means keeping them close and encouraging them to follow "tried and true" paths – or the "programming" to which Leah refers.

The course choice dilemma. I think many of us set out to take courses we *hope* will lead to a career (even though we often put more thought into decisions about the purchase of a car or house). In fairness, we likely have no idea that the career we think we might want when we're 20 years old, will not end up being the

---

[2] Susan Jeffers, *Feel the Fear and Do it Anyway* (New York, Random House Inc. 1987)

same one we want when we're 40 years of age, and beyond. Don't worry. You'll figure it out.

Recall Janice's explanation of how she ended up working in a pharmaceutical company—she'd taken typing and shorthand to prepare her for administrative work. Although she started out in an administrative role, Janice ultimately moved on to end her career in a senior management position.

The point is, it's important to take courses that interest you, or take courses you hope will lead to "something," or at the very least, take courses that "won't kill" you. I guarantee that whatever courses or education you pursue will not be a waste of time; all of our learning and experiences contribute in some way to shape our lives.

4. High school jobs can help determine a career path

Another important way we come to choose our work and career path is through the jobs we had in our youth, such as the after school, part-time job. I love hearing stories about part-time jobs people have had because they can teach such powerful life lessons. Here are a few examples of the ways in which part-time jobs can forever impact the trajectory of our work life:

Vivian described an incident that occurred when she was a teenager working at her part-time job. She feels the incident helped her figure out the path she ultimately choose to follow:

> *"So, what happened once was there was actually an accident, a workplace accident that happened right before closing. I think I was about 19 at the time.*

> *"Everybody was coming to me to say, 'Hey what should we do?' But this was a Saturday night, just before we closed and, really, it was all of us little kiddies left behind to close. I was completely unprepared. But, anyway, that incident never left me, and it was always in the back of my mind. I just never forgot how unprepared I was."*

Needless to say, Vivian recognized in that moment that health sciences would be her life's work.

Another story from Roger illustrates the ways in which we can be influenced by a part-time job:

> *"I had finished high school and my mother was bugging me to go to college. I told her I wanted to take time off and would go the next year. Actually, I had no intention of going but I knew she wouldn't accept that, so I told her I'd go next year. I ended up working in a construction job. The hours were long. It was dirty and noisy and, worst of all, it was the hardest work I'd ever done. I hated it. One day as I worked in the heat, operating a drilling-like tool, I realized I did not want to do this for the rest of my life, and college could not be this tough."*

Roger shared that he attended college that fall just as his mother had suggested. And, working in that summer job helped him recognize what he didn't want to be doing for the rest of his life.

5. A company ceases operations or files for bankruptcy/ restructuring, resulting in a sudden need to pivot

Another reality many people may need to confront at some point in their working life occurs when the organization they're working for goes out of business through bankruptcy or some other reason, or it undergoes downsizing and/or restructuring. When this occurs we are put in the position of needing to make choices about the next step along our career path.

Don't worry. You'll figure it out.

As I conducted the research for this book, I cannot tell you how many times I heard stories about closures, bankruptcies, mergers and acquisitions, restructuring and downsizing, all of which completely changed the career and work life trajectory of those involved. (There's lots more about this in Chapter 7.)

The Good News ...

The good news is, you are at a distinct point on your work-life journey. Regardless of where you are, or even how you arrived there, *you are right where you are supposed to* be.

I guarantee you that whatever path you have taken, you have accumulated wisdom, skills, knowledge and experience which will serve you well.

As you read this book, and take in the stories and experiences of others, I encourage you to begin to figure out what's next for you. Let it be your choice.

Recap of Key Points

1. Move forward with whatever skills, knowledge, and interests you possess. Don't worry. You'll be fine.

2. Work is a fundamental aspect of life; it provides elements which are critical to the well-being of human beings, including structure and purpose. Work comes in many forms, both paid and unpaid. Those without some form of work often feel at a loss to figure out their purpose.

3. Know the difference between a job and a career. Jobs are important and they do have purpose; perhaps just not your life's purpose. If you feel inspiration, passion, and excitement, you're probably following your career's path. Feeling work is all about "a-means-to-an-end" job, could mean you're on a "stepping stone" which will move you towards your life's work.

4. In truth, most of us had no idea what we wanted to become when we grew up. We were unwittingly influenced by many things including happenstance, parents, mentors, the courses we studied, and the part-time jobs we held. Pursue courses and activities that interest or inspire or challenge you.

5. There is no right or wrong path. You are right where you were meant to be. However, don't expect it to be easy; it's a "jungle gym." And don't worry. You'll figure it out.

6. Finally, the absolute most important point I want to make is this: the feeling that you're in a job or in a career is a choice. Let me explain: If I choose to perceive my work as uninspiring, boring, and perhaps even beneath me, I will likely behave in ways which reflect my boredom and disinterest. On the other hand, if I perceive my work to be interesting, challenging, fun and motivating, I am likely to

be a stellar employee and one co-workers and customers appreciate. How we perceive our work is a reflection of our mindset and attitude; we get to choose our mindset. And it's important we manage it.

Best Advice and Tips to Navigate Your Career Choice:

While researching this book, I asked people to tell me the best advice they could offer others to help them find their life's work? The following sage advice was generously offered:

- **Build a network of professionals**

    In whatever work you are considering, or are currently engaged, it is helpful to have a strong network. It's important to build relationships, and make sure you connect with others, both professionally and personally.

    Regardless of whatever point you are at in your career path, I encourage you to join associations relevant to your profession. Take advantage of the programs, services, professional development, and networking opportunities offered by the association. If you are considering starting your own business, connect with local, government-sponsored programs. Even if you are only considering a particular career path, join an association in that field as it is a way to evaluate whether it is a good fit for you. Do you feel interested, inspired, challenged etc., or do you find the topics boring and uninspiring? Consider the cost of joining an association an investment in finding your life's work. You don't have to become a lifetime member.

- **Get a mentor and/or be a mentor**

    The terms mentoring and coaching often get used interchangeably, which is somewhat misleading. While similar in the fact that they both support a person's development, they involve very different disciplines.

Mentoring consists of a relationship focused on supporting someone, or several people, with regard to growth and development. Often the mentoring relationship is intended to support the mentee's professional development, as, for example, in helping the individual become more proficient at report writing or presentation skills.

However, mentoring is not exclusive to work but applies to personal development, as well. The mentor has an area of expertise, which enables him or her to become a source of wisdom, teaching, and support, someone who observes and advises on specific actions or behaviour-related changes in daily work.

In contrast, coaching typically involves a relationship of finite duration, with a focus on strengthening or changing specific behaviours in the here-and-now. Coaching is less about instruction and more about helping individuals recognize their own capabilities and potential. Coaching involves active communication – questions, listening, and positive reinforcement to help individuals identify alternative ways of thinking about—and approaching—situations which enable them to make different choices and bring about more optimal outcomes.

Throughout my working life I have had the good fortune to benefit from numerous mentoring relationships. The arrangements have not been formal, meaning I did not "contract" with these individuals to teach, coach, and advise me about certain issues.

Rather, I understood that social learning, or modelling others' behaviour, is one the most powerful ways to learn and develop new skills. For example, at one point in my working life I worked under a leader who was highly skilled at diplomacy and tact. I had the highest level of respect for her ability to navigate even the most difficult situations exercising these two skills.

Look around you: are there people among your circle of friends, acquaintances, co-workers, bosses, partners, etc., who possess skills, qualities, positive traits, competencies, or knowledge which you admire and respect? If so, make a point of connecting with those people so you can learn from them.

Although mentoring offers mentees many benefits, the good news is that mentoring really is about creating "win-win" outcomes because there are many benefits to being a mentor. For example, "taking someone under your wing" is a fabulous way of giving back, particularly if you are in the later stage of your career.

Mentoring has the added benefit of helping to affirm our own expertise and skills in our respective professions. And it is a productive way to keep ourselves current in our profession.

- **Don't look for constant appreciation or "pats on the back;" rather learn to take gratification from—and feel great pride in—the work itself.**

A number of years ago I read a book called *Love the Work You're With: Find the Job You Always Wanted Without Leaving the One You Have* by Richard C. Whiteley[3]. I particularly recall the book because in the opening chapter Mr. Whiteley describes a man named

---

[3] Richard Whiteley, *Love the Work You're With: Find the Job You Always Wanted Without Leaving the One You Have* (New York, Henry Holt and Company, 2001)

Dave Kerpen, a snack vendor at a sports stadium. Mr.Whiteley says this man approached his work of selling popcorn and other snacks in an entertainment venue as though he absolutely loved what he was doing. Dave Kerpen was happy, fun loving, enthusiastic and genuinely thrilled to be doing his work. Fans in the stadium flocked to buy snacks from Dave because he had such a positive effect on others.

Wow! How many of us would be thrilled doing a job that required us to lug a heavy tray up and down stairs selling snacks to loud, rambunctious people? Mr. Whiteley makes the point that, "selling Crunch'n Munch may not be Dave Kerpen's ultimate dream job—he graduated from Boston University with a double major—but because he infuses it with "dream job" spirit, it delivers great rewards.

It is meaningful because he makes others happy. It gives him recognition because only he can do what he does in the way he does it. It makes him productive. And obviously it brings him joy."

In other words, do not seek constant recognition and appreciation from others. If you apply yourself and approach work and life with a positive attitude, a sense of fun and yes, even gratitude for whatever you are doing, it can feel like as much like a dream job to you as Dave Kerpen's does to him.

Mr. Whiteley makes the wise observation that "jobs don't have spirit ... people do"[4] and it's this spirit, which delivers dream job rewards – meaning, recognition, and purpose to feed our souls.

---

[4] Whitely *Love the Work You're With:* (New York, Henry Holt and Company, 2001), P.3

Recognize the Path of Least Resistance

The path of least resistance was introduced earlier in the chapter. It is what Leah characterized as "programming" or conforming to expectations. Of course, our loved ones only want the very best for us, and they give advice to help keep us safe and protected from life's struggles.

In reality, when we choose the path of least resistance it tends to lead to – Nowhere. The path of least resistance often does not lead to a life of meaning, passion and purpose. So, parents, let your offspring find their way. Encourage them to figure it out for themselves. Trust in them. Believe that he or she or they will be fine.

If you're on the path of least resistance, look around and ask yourself "is this taking me in the direction I want to be going?" If your answer is "yes," then carry on. But, if you're not sure you're headed in the right direction, I encourage you to consider your options. (more on this idea in chapters ahead!)

- **Don't Worry. You'll Figure it Out.**

If I have learned anything over the course of my working life, and during the many conversations I always enjoy having with others about their work, I have become absolutely convinced that, as one woman put it, "you don't need to know all the answers," and, "there are no mistakes." Don't worry. You will figure it out. Here's how another person articulated this idea: "You will come up against many obstacles and many of them will be you. Embrace every one and know they are not unsolvable."

Chapter 2

The Changing Nature of Work and Workplaces

> ***Real happiness is not obtained through self-gratification but through fidelity to a worthy purpose.***
>
> **—Helen Keller**

Over the years of my research I have had many conversations with people about their careers and their work lives. I've repeatedly heard people say they wish they had known more about work and workplaces before they began their work-life journey because they had absolutely no idea what to expect.

One woman told me that when she began her career, like most of us, she felt confused about "those basic things you think everybody should know but they actually don't." This chapter describes the changing landscape of work and workplaces.

Some people may find this chapter to be a bit of a reality check and in the spirit of exploration I invite you to complete the following exercise:

Exercise:

Imagine you fell asleep and awakened on a workday from the era of your childhood. For example, if you are 30 years old now, imagine a workday from 25 or 30 years ago. What jobs exist today that did not exist then? What jobs were present when you were a child but have become extinct or obsolete?

I have done this exercise with many different audiences and can tell you the list of changes people have observed over the past 20 or 30 years, or more, can be quite long. The jobs or types of work which have become extinct or obsolete include:

- Door-to-door milk delivery services

- Door-to-door sales of merchandise such as encyclopedias, vacuum cleaners, and household products

- Journalists producing a local daily newspaper

- "Paper boys" responsible for delivering the daily paper

- Switchboard operators

- Gas station attendants who pumped your gas for you (most stations are now self-service)

- Fast food servers who brought your meal to your car on a tray

- Many others!

Creating Your Career / Denise O'Brien

What's in a Job Title?

The list of job titles that exist today but did not exist in the past is lengthy and the titles are much more imaginative than they ever used to be. Titles such as, Chief Happiness Officer, Director of First Impressions, Chief Recognition Officer, and Director of Innovation are just a few of the most recent trends.

Nowadays, many companies have become far more generous (and creative) with job titles, and a primary reason is to enable them to recruit and retain top talent.

For example, during my research, one person shared that she had a job with a "big, important title" which she was reluctant to give up because she had worked hard and ascended the corporate ladder; the title represented status and power.

As I have come to understand over the course of my career, status and power can become a powerful "drug" that keeps us tied to work that does not always give us purpose or feed our soul.

With the number of small businesses and start-ups rapidly increasing, job titles are one of the few ways a company low on money can attract potential candidates. In other words, gone are the days of common or "standardized" job titles. Before you accept a job and the respective title it carries, consider asking for minor "tweaks" to the title to make it more relevant.

For example, consider integrating some of the terminology common in your field in to your job title. A few years ago, I noticed the word "Strategic" had begun to show up in job titles, which in itself was perhaps a way of giving the appearance of greater relevance.

A Note of Caution: during my research people shared examples of getting pigeon-holed by job titles which did not reflect their duties. The Merriam-Webster dictionary defines pigeon-holing as "to unfairly think of or describe (someone or something) as belonging to a particular group, having only a particular skill, etc."[5]

One's job title can (and should) inform people about such issues as the nature of the work you perform, your duties, your scope of authority and your level of experience. Ensure your job title is a current reflection of your duties, responsibilities and capabilities to avoid being pigeon-holed.

Diversity

While work activities, job descriptions and titles have changed and evolved over the years there have also been significant changes within our workplaces. No matter where you are in your work life journey, you can expect to be working in a very diverse workplace.

This is good news, as there are many benefits to working in a diverse and inclusive workplace. Here are just some of the reasons why we should strive to build and nurture diversity in our workplaces:

- **Diversity makes a variety of different perspectives available to us**

    Diversity offers opportunities to gain different perspectives for new ways of thinking, and greater capacity for problem solving which ultimately lead to more optimal outcomes.

---

[5] Merriam-Webster Dictionary, https://www.merriam-webster

Diversity in the workplace means employees will have different personal characteristics and backgrounds, and they are likely to have a variety of skills and experiences.

- **It increases creativity**

   People from diverse backgrounds bring unique and rich experiences and perspectives to the workplace and exposure to this variety leads to heightened levels of creativity. It's been my experience that when you put people together who see the same thing in different ways, you create greater opportunities to generate synergistic energy which lends itself to a culture of creativity.

- **It enables greater innovation**

   In a diverse workplace, employees are exposed to multiple perspectives and worldviews. Combining these various perspectives creates a greater potential for people to come together in novel ways, and results in a greater overall willingness to take a few risks and do some "out of the box" thinking. Innovation and new ideas are the natural by-product of this approach.

- **Diversity allows for faster problem-solving**

   Harvard Business Review found that diverse teams are able to solve problems faster than people who think the same (this is known as "group think.").[6] What's more,

---

[6] Alison Reynolds and David Lewis, "Teams solve problems faster when they're more cognitively diverse," *Harvard Business Review*

people from varied backgrounds have different experiences and views, which is why they are able to bring diverse solutions to the table. Thus, the best solution can be chosen sooner, which leads to faster problem-solving.

- **It facilitates better decisions**

    Research has found a direct link between workplace diversity and decision-making. In particular, when diverse teams make a business decision, they tend to outperform individual decision-makers up to 87% of the time.[7]

    Engaging and collaborating with individuals from a range of backgrounds and perspectives creates opportunities for more solutions, which leads to more informed and highly improved decision-making processes and results.

- **It allows for bigger profits**

    McKinsey & Company, a global management consulting firm, conducted research which included 180 companies in France, Germany, the United Kingdom, and the United States.[8] They found that companies with more diverse top teams were also top financial performers, and thus more competitive.

---

[7] 2017, "Diversity drives better decisions," *People Management*, https://www.peoplemanagement.co.uk/experts/research/diversity

[8] Thomas Barta, Markus Kleiner, and Tilo Neumann, "Is there a payoff from top-team diversity?", *McKinsey and Company*

- **It increases employee engagement**

    Professional Services Firm Deloitte conducted research that captured the views and experiences of 1,550 employees in three large Australian businesses operating in manufacturing, retail, and healthcare.

    The research showed that engagement is an outcome of diversity and inclusion.[9] The link between workplace diversity and employee engagement is pretty clear: when employees feel included, they are more invested in the outcomes—which leads to higher levels of engagement.

- **Diversity reduces employee turnover**

    Companies with a diverse workforce are generally more inclusive of different individual characteristics and perspectives. Diverse and inclusive workplaces are more likely to be ones in which all employees feel generally accepted and valued. This makes them happier and less likely to leave.

- **It bolsters a company's reputation for being a good corporate citizen**

    In other words, organizations which are dedicated to building and promoting diversity in the workplace are seen as good, more human, and more socially responsible organizations.

---

[9] Giam Swiegers and Karen Toohey, "Waiter is that inclusion in my soup? A new recipe to improve business performance," Victorian Equal Opportunity and Human Rights Commission

- **It helps attract great talent**

    Diversity in the workplace boosts a company's brand and presents a company as a more desirable place to work. Workplace diversity is an especially beneficial asset for attracting top talent from diverse talent pools.

    Research conducted by Glassdoor found that as many as 67% of job seekers feel a diverse workforce is important to them when they are considering job opportunities.[10]

As you can see, there are many benefits to embracing workplace diversity. So, if I have sold you on the "What's in it for me?" aspect of the idea (WIFM), let me share examples of the ways in which diversity is now reflected in our workplaces.

Today's work environments are much more diverse in a variety of ways – in terms of race, education, gender, and age.

Racial Diversity
According to Statistics Canada, in May 2016, approximately 17.2 million people were employed in Canadian workplaces. Of this employed population, immigrants accounted for 23.4% of the labour force (up from 21.2% in 2006).[i] As noted above, racial diversity within our workplace offers many opportunities to leverage.

Educaional Diversity
As workplaces have become much more racially diverse with new immigrants, workplaces have reaped the benefits by way of the educational backgrounds many have brought to our

---

[10] "What job seekers really think about your diversity and inclusion stats," *Glassdoor*

Canadian workplaces. For example, between 2001 and 2011 approximately 41% of those who immigrated to Canada held a university degree.[11]

In addition to welcoming highly educated immigrants, as a society Canadians generally are pursuing higher levels of education. In 2014, for instance, nearly 30% of all Canadian adults held a university degree.[12] Many of those who haven't chosen a university program have pursued post-secondary education at college to obtain diplomas and certificates. This has positioned many workplaces to become more "knowledge centric" and enabled them to leverage changing societal demands for goods and services.

Gender Diversity

For those of us who grew up in the 1970s and beyond, it will come as no surprise to learn women continue to be highly represented in our workplaces. Statistics indicate that in 2018, for example women 15 years and older represented nearly half (47.7%) of the Canadian labour force. This represents a 30% increase from 1976 at which time only approximately 37.1% of the Canadian labour force was female.[13]

Age Diversity

For the first time ever, we have five generations in the workforce, each with different perspectives, expectations, and

---

[11] "Percentage of 25 to 64 year olds in population with a university degree," **University of Waterloo**

[12] **"Differences in the location of study of university-educated immigrants,"** Statistics Canada

[13] "Women in the workforce – Canada: Quick take," *Catalyst*

experiences – all of which need to be managed within the workplace. This is not an easy challenge! The generations include:

1. The Silent Generation of people born between 1925 and 1945
2. Baby Boomers born between 1946 and 1964
3. Generation Xers born between 1965 and 1980
4. Millennials, who were born between 1981 and 2001 and
5. Members of Generation Z, who were born after 2001

Researchers estimate that moving into 2020 and beyond, as the Silent Generation and Baby Boomers exit the workplace, Millennials will comprise as much as 50% of the global workforce. Looking forward to 2025, we can expect approximately 75% of the global workforce will come from the Millennial generation. [14]

As we say goodbye to the Silent Generation and the Baby Boom generation, we will see a few trends in our workplaces which we can attribute to the emerging Millennial demographic:

- **More workplace tech**
  Millennials (and those in Generation Z) grew up with technology, mobile apps, and innovative platforms. They are often the first ones Baby Boomers reach out to for help when they have a computer or internet problem. It should come as no surprise if your company invests in more devices and technologies as Millennials and Generation Zers assume their lead in the workforce.

---

[14] Peter Economy, "The millennial workplace of the future is almost here ... these 3 things are about to change big time," *Inc.*

Creating Your Career / Denise O'Brien

Also, we should expect to see changes in the ways individuals interface and share information. For example, in-person meetings will continue to decline as video conferencing continues to become more popular. Again, this should come as no surprise!

One thing the Coronavirus pandemic has highlighted for many of us is how dependent we have become upon technologies which enable us to meet virtually. During this unprecedented time of social isolation, many of us would be "lost" without it.

If you are a Millennial or a member of Generation Z reading this book, you are likely feeling quite pleased to learn the integration of more technology into workplaces will definitely continue to trend upwards in the coming years.

So, if you are technologically savvy you are well positioned to find your niche in the workplace.

On the other hand, if technology is "not your thing" be forewarned that you may find it more challenging to be sustained in work environments that are becoming more and more dependent on technology.

- **Collaboration will be the norm**
  Millennials and Generation Zers are also experts at using social networks and collaborative tools like Wikipedia to share ideas and innovations. Many people from these generations grew up attending schools in which classroom activities and assignments were structured around teamwork, participation, and a significant amount of collaboration.

Thus, many learned the concepts of working together from an early age, and beyond. In many organizations, the emphasis on teamwork and collaboration is already evident, with the creation of open office layouts in which co-workers can easily and frequently interact and share ideas.

- **Flexibility, flexibility, flexibility**
  Although collaboration and teamwork will continue to be the norm, apparent within the Millennial and Generation Z generations is an emerging trend towards greater levels of autonomy, independence and the ability to complete work—anytime and from anywhere without "being tied" to a work location.

  In other words, "tell me what needs to be done and then give me the freedom and flexibility to complete it" without too many restrictions.

  My experiences tell me there is a definite interest in being able to "do my work anytime and from anywhere."

  Statistics Canada issued a 2018 study that provides some insight into the association between job flexibility and job satisfaction in Canadians aged 18 to 64. This study examined four aspects of job flexibility including:

  - the order of work (or the sequence of tasks)
  - how the work is done
  - the speed of work and
  - the hours of work

  In both men and women, control over the hours of work was most strongly associated with job satisfaction. This association was even stronger among younger individuals.[15]

As I write this book the concept of flexibility, particularly around working remotely ("working from home") is being practiced by many workplaces to protect worker health and safety as a result of the 2020 Coronavirus pandemic.

Once the dust has settled, it will be interesting to see whether organizations will continue to support "working from home" policies. Perhaps the pandemic will be the push many workplaces needed to help them realize the potential benefits of finding more creative ways to complete work.

- **Short-term "gigs"**
  Compared to the traditional idea of full-time work, Millennials have indicated that freelance and contract work that commonly comprise what we call the "gig economy" are appealing. Short-term gigs are very much a Millennial and Gen Z trend and not one the Baby Boom generation has typically embraced.

  The primary reason this approach to work has not held appeal to the typical Baby Boomer is that short term gigs offer little or no security. Baby Boomers, do not be too hasty! I strongly encourage this generation to consider the benefits of short-term work activities and projects, even in post-retirement as a worthwhile pursuit. (More about this in Chapter 8.)

---

[15] Steve Martin, "The association between job flexibility and job satisfaction," *Statistics Canada*

How Can Employers Attract and Retain Millennials?

Millennials and the members of Generation Z will influence many workplace changes and I was curious about the trends that potentially lay ahead for employers who recruit and retain talent from among these generations. I found Deloitte's Global Millennial Survey, *Societal Discord and Technological Transformation Create a "Generation Disrupted*,[16] to be most informative. The study provides a nice summary of the expected challenges facing employers given the emerging dominance of Millennial and Gen Z workers in the workplace.

For instance, one of the most startling findings from this report was that 49% of the Millennials surveyed would quit their jobs in the next two years if they could.

Roughly a quarter of those same individuals reported leaving an employer in the past 24 months. The top reasons cited by these employees for leaving their employment included dissatisfaction with pay, and a lack of advancement and professional development opportunities. In light of these findings, there is a real risk employers will have difficulty maintaining a stable workforce in the future.

Technological Advances

In addition to becoming accustomed to creative job titles and descriptions, and greater levels of diversity and inclusion, in future we can all expect to be working in workplaces which rely heavily on technology. For example, think about how quickly we have all become dependent upon our smart phones.

I recall the first cellular phones. They were large, clunky devices which were not easy to carry. They had limited

---

[16] "The Deloitte Global Millennial Survey 2019," *Deloitte*

functionality and they were extremely costly to purchase and use. I also remember another type of device called a handheld organizer, of which the "palm pilot" was one of the most prominent examples. They quickly became obsolete.

It's safe to assume technology will continue to become increasingly sophisticated, and important, in the conduct of our work. The evolution continues.

When the iPhone shipped to customers on June 29, 2007, the first generation of the device that would change the world was missing a lot of what we now expect in a smart phone, but it was a huge leap forward from the original cell phone technology and handheld organizer devices which had already hit the market.

The iPhone marked the debut of the touchscreen, which would soon become standard in the category. Sure, there had been smartphones available from established manufacturers before, but they had physical keyboards and a much smaller screen.

According to a 2018 survey conducted by Consumer Technology Association approximately 86% of Canadians own a smartphone.[17]

Plus,
- Canadians have, on average, 80 apps on their phone
- They use, on average, nine apps per day
- They use, on average, 30 apps per month
- The app industry is a billion-dollar industry that continues to grow exponentially

---

[17] Ian Hardy, "86 percent of Canadians own a Smartphone Says CTA Report," *Mobile Syrup*

This is inevitably having an impact on the world of work. What's more, as artificial intelligence (AI) continues to evolve, we can expect to see even greater reliance on automation and technology.

If you are just starting out on your career path, are currently employed, or are looking to make a different choice in your employment path you might be interested in some of the components that currently make up a typical workplace:

The Typical Workplace is Lean and Agile
Cutbacks, downsizing, rightsizing, restructuring, bankruptcy, mergers and acquisitions—not to mention the massive economic recalibration caused by the global pandemic—have left the organizations still standing very lean indeed.

Departments, divisions, lines of business and staff have been eliminated due to economic exigencies.

Many organizations are focused on "doing more with less." The Lean Enterprise model was introduced to the world by Toyota in the 1970s but did not really take off in North America until well into the 1980s and early 90s.

Since then, it has fuelled changes in organizations around the world, particularly, but not exclusively, in manufacturing and product development.

The Key Principles of "Lean Thinking" are:

1. Define value from the customer's perspective.

2. Identify internal activities and processes that add value for the customer and identify linkages between them (the value chain).

3. Eliminate non-value-added activities (or waste) across the organization.

4. Reduce waste and inefficiencies in support (i.e. overhead) functions.

The Lean approach has enabled many organizations to respond more rapidly to the marketplace by reducing cycle time, developing mass customization processes, and supporting continual change and innovation.

While it does increase efficiencies and cost-savings, this Lean approach has also brought about the elimination of many jobs.

Adopting Lean principles and Lean thinking has led to widespread change in organizational structure to improve the efficiency of internal processes, with a goal of eliminating waste and defining customer value.

These changes have been supported, and continue to be supported, by expanding technologies such as the internet, mobile computing, digitalization, AI and a variety of other communication-related innovations.

Key organizational characteristics that support a Lean environment include:

A Reduced Hierarchical Structure

Hierarchies are cumbersome and cannot respond quickly to changing market demands, such as pressures for reduced cycle time and continuous innovation.

Hierarchies have been—and continue to be—replaced by cross-unit organizational groupings with fewer layers and more decentralized decision making.

Blurred Boundaries

When organizations become more laterally structured boundaries break down as different parts of the organization need to work more effectively together. Boundaries between departments as well as between job categories (manager, professional, technical) become looser and there is a greater need for task- and knowledge-sharing.

Teams as Basic Building Blocks

The move towards a team-based organizational structure results from pressures to make rapid decisions, reduce inefficiencies, and continually improve work processes. Distribution of shared responsibilities across the team mitigates risks: in the event someone leaves the team the goods or services can still be produced.

Evolving Management Styles

In effectively managed workplaces, employees are no longer being "policed" to ensure they comply with rules and orders. Rather, leaders now collaborate to establish organizational purpose, mission and strategic goals.

The blurring of boundaries also affects organizational roles. As employees gain more autonomy, managers move away from being technical experts and commanders to become more social supporters and coaches.

Continuous Change

I repeatedly hear "the only thing that is constant is change." Whichever point you are at on your work-life journey I highly recommend you apply yourself to learn more about navigating change. The importance of knowing how to navigate change should be evident for those of you whose work was impacted by COVID-19.

One gentleman I spoke with about how his work and life were changed by the pandemic said this:

> "For years my work has required me to hop on planes, fly to different places and engage with different audiences. In less than 24-hours with the imposition of social isolation rules and flight restrictions my work had changed. I was essentially 'out of work' and without an income. I went into a funk. I had to re-invent myself from my apartment."

Fortunately, this person was familiar with change principles and was able to adapt to changing circumstances. Don't delay. Access information to help you develop your "change muscles." There are many wonderful resources available to help you and I've included many of them throughout this book.

The bottom-line is this: the typical workplace has embraced "lean" principles which are essentially about "doing more with less." Thus, it is even more important to become adept at navigating change and, of course, embracing principles of teamwork.

How Work is Changing for Individuals

Over the past two decades, a new pattern of work has been emerging as the knowledge economy realizes the full potential of new technologies and new organizational models. The changes fall into the following areas:

- There is an increased need for higher levels of education because of the disappearance of the industrial era and the growth of knowledge and digital economies.

- There is greater emphasis on the importance of social and emotional intelligence in building relationships (more about this in Chapter 3).

- There is a new "psychological contract" between employees and employers. (Read on, the psychological contract is described later in this chapter.)

- Changes are being made to process and place, in other words where, when, and how work is being done. And, as noted earlier, perhaps the 2020 Coronavirus pandemic will move the pendulum even further as workplaces figure out how to get work done remotely.

The Knowledge Worker

I mentioned earlier the trend towards higher levels of education, which is being driven by the need for "knowledge" workers. In other words, there is a growing need for workers to be more functionally and cognitively fluid, and able to work across many kinds of tasks and situations. The broader span of work—brought about by changes in organizational structure—has also created new demands. In other words, as I mentioned earlier, there is an emphasis on "doing more with less."

Employees today need to know more, not only to do their jobs and tasks but also to work effectively with others on the team. Many knowledge-based tasks require sound analytical and judgment skills to carry out work that is more novel, and context based, with few rules and structured ways of working.

Although demands for high cognitive skills are especially prominent in professional, technical, and managerial jobs, even administrative tasks require more independent decision making.

Not only do employees need to keep their technology skills up-to-date, they need to be continuous learners in their knowledge fields, and also to be more familiar with business strategy. Taking time to read and attend educational classes is no longer a prerequisite for only a few, it is essential for all workers.

Rosabeth Moss Kanter argues that "kaleidoscope thinking"[18]—the ability to see alternative angles and perspectives and to create new patterns of thinking that fuel innovation—will be a highly-valued and necessary competence in the changing landscape of work. In future, employees will need to be able to synthesize unrelated ideas effectively and efficiently in order to make the cognitive leaps that underpin innovation.

Caution: Cognitive Overload Ahead

Vastly increased access to information has paradoxically made work both easier and more difficult. The ease comes from the fact that we can now rapidly locate and download information from diverse sources. The difficulty comes from the need to consume and make sense of the vast quantity of new information that is coming at us faster. In other words, we are not machines, yet we are expected to process information as quickly as they do.

Beware: information overload coupled with time pressures and increased work complexity can lead to cognitive overload. A moderate degree of cognitive overload tends to

---

[18] Rosabeth Moss Kanter, 10th Anniversary Essays on Jobs and Social Innovation, *Stanford Social Innovation Review*

feel like a welcome challenge, stimulating and almost re-energizing us. However, ongoing and continuous cognitive overload can bring on symptoms of stress, the inability to concentrate, a tendency towards multitasking, a habit of switching tasks, and an inclination to focus on what is easy to do quickly, rather than what is important. Longer periods of cognitive overload may ultimately lead to burnout.

Burnout

The phenomenon of burnout is not new. The Canadian Psychological Association has prepared a straightforward and helpful resource entitled, "Psychology Works Fact Sheet: Burnout"[19] in which burnout is defined as psychological strain that is brought about by prolonged chronic job stressors which exceed an individual's capacity to cope.

The fact sheet indicates that exhaustion, cynicism and inefficacy are the three key dimensions of the burnout experience. We all feel wiped out from time to time but if you are experiencing burnout, the *exhaustion* is overwhelming – you feel tired almost all of the time, both physically and emotionally.

No one wants or chooses the experience of burnout. People would prefer to be engaged and have enough resources to keep up with the demands of their day-to-day lives.

It is important to keep in mind that burnout is *not* just an individual problem; it is the result of factors in the work environment.

We experience stress when the demands we face – physical, emotional, or otherwise – are greater than the resources we have. Our personal stressors can make us more likely to experience burnout – if we are going through personal

---

[19] Canadian Psychological Association, *Psychology Works Factsheet: Burnout*, (Ottawa, 2020)

health or relationship challenges, we are often more vulnerable to the impacts of work stressors.

How do you know if you are experiencing burnout?

According to the Canadian Psychological Association, burnout tends to emerge over time and is associated with changes in how you approach your life, in such areas as:

- **Emotions and Motivation**
    - Loss of motivation about work; low excitement and engagement
    - Decreased job satisfaction
    - Pronounced irritability, spontaneous anger
    - Anxiety, worry, insecurity
    - Feeling alone in the world; a desire to isolate oneself
    - Feelings of incompetence and failure; a drop in self-confidence
    - Frustration or anger at oneself

- **Thoughts**
    - Negative thoughts related to one's job
    - Increased focus on errors, mistakes and failures
    - Cynicism over others' intentions
    - Increased detachment from one's job

- Negative or inappropriate attitudes towards clients, customers or colleagues
- Loss of idealism; greater intention to leave the job
- Difficulties with concentration, memory, judgment, decision-making

- **Behaviour**
    - Difficulty producing the results you want or intend at work
    - Lower productivity or accomplishment; inefficiency
    - Procrastination
    - Withdrawal and social isolation
    - Absenteeism

- **Body/Physical Well Being**
    - Persistent fatigue and exhaustion; feeling tired most of the time; low energy; feeling "worn out"
    - Pain (headaches, backaches); sore muscles
    - Increased susceptibility to cold, flus and infections

- Sleep problems (difficulty falling or staying asleep, or early morning awakenings)
- Gastrointestinal symptoms (digestive problems, ulcers); irritable bowel symptoms; changes in appetite or weight
- Skin problems (hives, eczema)

Stay tuned in and notice when you're feeling overwhelmed at work. As mentioned earlier, burnout is not something that happens overnight. Rather, when we feel more and more overwhelmed with the demands placed upon us and our ability to juggle all we have on our plates is stretched too thin, we're heading down an unhealthy path that will not serve us well.

Competencies to be Leveraged

As you can see, the landscape of the workplace is changing, and it will continue to change. People often ask me what competencies they need to thrive in the changing workplace. Here are a few basics:

- **Social and Emotional Intelligence**

    A report on the changing nature of work prepared by the National Research Council [20] called attention to the important interpersonal and relationship development aspects of work. As collaboration and collective activity become more prevalent, workers need well-developed social and emotional intelligence skills.

---

[20] Committee on Techniques for the Enhancement of Human Performance: Occupational Analysis, "The Changing Nature of Work: Implications for Occupational Analysis" (Washington, National Academy Press, 1999)

With our increased reliance on technology it may seem incongruent that social and emotional intelligence skills are considered to be essential competencies to be effective in the landscape of an ever-changing workplace. Look around, for example, as you are walking down the street or riding on public transit and notice the number of people who are interacting with their personal devices.

I even notice people travelling in vehicles in which the driver is focused on the road while the passenger interacts with a smart phone or tablet. Those with young children might find they never get in the car for a long trip without some form of technology to keep young minds entertained.

Rarely are people actually engaged in conversations. This is the reality in workplaces, as well, and it can lead to interpersonal challenges at work. Because social and emotional intelligence are such important aspects of navigating work, I have included a more fulsome discussion of these topics in Chapter 3.

- **Teamwork and Collaboration**

    Conflict resolution and negotiation skills are essential to collaborative work. Conflicts often occur over group goals, work methods, workloads, and personality and work style differences. My own experience has confirmed that team members with good conflict and negotiation skills—and a high level of emotional intelligence—are well equipped to deal with problems.

    Plus, the ability to listen and be respectful of different perspectives goes a long way towards resolving issues in mutually beneficial ways. The book, *Building Smart*

Teams, by Carol Beatty and Brenda Barker Scott, provides insight into the ways in which workplaces are now structured around a framework of teamwork and collaboration.[21]

- **Relationship Development and Networking**

    People can build reciprocity and trust if they are willing and able to listen, share important information, fulfill on promises, and stay open to the influence of others.

    When workers trust one another, they are more committed to attaining mutual goals, more likely to help one another through difficulties, and more willing to share and develop new ideas. Relationship development is really about to getting along with others.

    While this competency is essential to work effectively within most organizations it's also been identified by Dr. Thomas Stanley in his book *The Millionaire Mind*[22] to be on the list of the top five factors to which millionaires attribute their financial success.

- **Learning and Growth**

    Many organizations strive to create conditions in which employees learn through formal training and their relationships with co-workers. Learning relationships are built on respect, synergy, give-and-take, joint problem

---

[21] Carol Beatty and Brenda Barker Scott, *Building smart teams: A roadmap to high performance*, (Thousand Oaks, Sage Publications Ltd., 2004)

[22] Thomas Stanley, *The Millionaire Mind* (Rosetta Books, 2010)

solving, learning from mistakes, sharing insights, and working closely together.

I am a huge fan of mentoring relationships because—as pointed out in Chapter 1—mentoring creates a win-win situation.

Leadership Competencies

While researching this book, I had the good fortune to interview Dr. Benoit Hardy Vallee, Associate Partner, Talent and Engagement, at IBM Services. I asked him this question:

"Given the increasing reliance on technology and automation, as well as the pace of change, what are the 10 Key Leadership Competencies required to lead during these turbulent times?"

Here is what Vallee identified as important:

1. The Capacity for behaving with Integrity - – to use big data, technology and AI wisely to augment human capacity rather than replace or eliminate it
2. Critical thinking – work is cognitively more demanding
3. Strategic thinking
4. Collaboration
5. Deep empathy
6. Inter-cultural sensitivity
7. Openness to diversity
8. Absolute focus on talent
9. Willingness to be a continuous learner
10. MUST EMBRACE TECHNOLOGY

So, if you aspire to be an effective leader, make it your practice to continue to develop these invaluable competencies. Trust me, you and your workplace will be much better served.

Technology's Impact on Jobs/Work/Careers

So, which jobs are expected to be impacted the most by technologies, including artificial intelligence? Researchers at Oxford University estimated in 2013 that 47% of jobs could be automated within the next decade or two.[23]

Other research from 2016 conducted at the Organization for Economic Cooperation and Development (OECD) [24] used an alternate model to produce an estimate. Interestingly, the results from this study directly contradict the Oxford study findings and estimate only 9% of jobs were at high risk of automation.

Still other research conducted by McKinsey Global Institute landed somewhere in the middle. As you can see, a lot of researchers are trying to figure out the answer to the questions "How will technology impact jobs?" And, "Is my work actually at risk of being automated?" Unfortunately, it would seem the answers to these questions are yet to be determined.

In my quest to find out which jobs might be impacted or potentially eliminated, I looked to the work of Dr. Kai-Fu Lee. A highly regarded expert on AI, Dr. Lee provides insight on these questions in his book "AI Super-Powers: China, Silicon Valley and the New World Order."

---

[23] C. Frey and M. Osborne, "The Future of Employment: How Susceptible Are Jobs to Automation," *Oxford Martin Programme on Technology and Employment*, September 17, 2013

[24] Melanie Arntz, Terry Gregory, and Ulrich Zierahn, "The Risk of Automation for Jobs in OECD Countries: A Comparative Analysis," *OECD Social, Employment, and Migration Working Papers, no189, May 14, 2016,*

In his book, Dr. Lee segregates the potential for job loss for cognitive and physical labour jobs into four distinct areas across an X-Y continuum. These areas include Danger Zone, Slow Creep, Human Veneer, and Safe Zone[25].

1. **Jobs in what Dr. Lee calls the Danger Zone have low relationship/personal care elements and low dexterity requirements.** He asserts that these jobs are in imminent danger of being replaced—or at least heavily augmented—with automation, particularly via AI. They include:

Cognitive Labour	**Physical Labour**
Telemarketer	Teller/Casher
Customer loan underwriter	Fast food preparer
Basic translator	Restaurant cook
Insurance adjuster	Garment factory worker
Personal tax preparer	Dishwasher
Customer service representative	Fruit harvester
	Truck driver
	Assembly line worker

2. **Jobs in the Slow Creep Zone (meaning gradually these functions will be replaced or at least heavily augmented by automation) include:**

Cognitive Labour	**Physical Labour**
Graphic designer	Nightwatch security guard
Legal/financial analyst	Plumber
Scientist	Home construction/finishing work
Artist	
Columnist	Taxi driver
	House cleaner

---

[25] Kai-Fu Lee, *AI Super-powers China, Silicon Valley and the new world order* (Boston, Houghton Mifflin Harcourt, 2018)

Creating Your Career / Denise O'Brien

As you read the above lists of jobs that technology will inevitably change it may seem hard to imagine.

Think about the job of house cleaner. Can you ever imagine a time when your house could be cleaned with an automated device?

I definitely want to be first on the list for this device when it's available!) In reality, housework has been, and will continue to be heavily dependent upon technology and automation.

For example, I have a Roomba which I program to vacuum my house at convenient times. I no longer get on my hands and knees to wash my floors as I have a device that automatically releases water and steam. I can ask Google or Alexa to turn on my washing machine and oven.

While I still have household chores to do, I do them much differently than the way my mother did because I have much more sophisticated gizmos to help me get them done.

3. **Human Veneer – jobs in this category are a little safer because there is a social-orientation towards meeting individual customer needs.** However, think about it: even jobs which require social interaction could be augmented even further with technology.

Cognitive Labour	Physical Labour
Wedding planner	Bartender
Teacher	Caterer
Doctor (General Practitioner)	Luxury hotel receptionist
Tour guide	Café waiter
Financial planner	

Here's an example of how this might increasingly look: I recently visited an organization that provides a health care service and found there was no receptionist sitting in the reception area.

There was, however, an automated technological device that sensed movement and said something like "Good afternoon. I'm Amy. Welcome to ABC Healthcare. How may I help you this afternoon?"

I found it ironic that a healthcare organization, in the business of human service, had eliminated the receptionist's position and installed an automated system instead.

4. **In the changing landscape of work and how it gets done Dr. Lee also identifies work that is, at least for now, in the Safe Zone.** This category includes jobs which require a high degree of social dexterity, are very individual in nature, and take place in what he refers to as an "unstructured environment."

Cognitive Labour	Physical Labour
Social worker	Dog trainer
Criminal defense attorney	Physical therapist
Public Relations **director**	Hair stylist
Psychiatrist	Elderly home caretaker
Concierge	

Deborah Bubb, VP and Chief Leadership, Learning & Inclusion Officer @ IBM offered the following[26] questions to ponder to help inform yourself about which jobs/work/careers

---

[26] Neil Morelli ,"Artificial intelligence in talent assessment and selection," *SIOP White Paper Series*

we can expect to be impacted by automation in the coming years:

- What tasks would be better if they were done 24/7?
- What tasks would be better if they were able to be completed at maximum efficiency?
- What tasks would benefit from greater consistency?
- What would be possible if we leveraged broader expertise to see beyond our current limits?

Your answers to the above questions are all good candidates for AI!

It is pretty evident much about the landscape of work has changed and will continue to change. It is a very exciting time to be on the work-life journey.

One final and important topic I want to include about the changing landscape of work is perhaps a bit of a reality check for those who are hoping to secure one job or career for life. There really is no such thing as "a job for life." The next section describes the "psychological contract" we should anticipate sharing with our employer(s).

The New Psychological Contract

In the new work context, the informal "psychological contract" between workers and employers—i.e. what each expects of the other—focuses on competency development, continuous learning and work/life balance.

By contrast, the old psychological contract was all about job security and steady upward advancement within the same company. Today's reality is that few workers should expect lifelong employment in a single company.

My own experience and the wisdom of social science practitioners can be boiled down into some general observations I put forward for your consideration:

Corporate Indifference. Today's employees are more invested in "psychological self-determination" than ever before. These individuals are invested in participation, expression, identity, and quality of life – *now*. While many organizations ascribe to these values in practice, as mentioned earlier, they tend to embrace lean principles with a focus on practical demands such as reducing costs and maximizing efficiencies.

In other words, some organizations stress the desirability of "doing more with less" while at the same time, these same organizations are telling employees to be mindful of their mental health. In my experience, attending a yoga class offered by the workplace at lunchtime will not protect me from experiencing symptoms of burnout if I am feeling chronically overwhelmed by the demands of my work.

At times, it may feel like "corporate indifference" but it is more likely that the organization is doing the best it can.

Reduced Loyalty and Commitment. With little, or at least *reduced* expectations for advancement (more about this in Chapter 6), individuals are likely to feel less committed to their organization's goals. Rather, energy and attention often get re-directed to personal learning and development in pursuit of personal goals.

In other words, since the organization likely will not provide me with a "job for life," I need to be on the lookout for the skills and knowledge I will need to be able to market myself to my next employers.

This is likely not news to anyone! In fact, many books published in the early 1990s emphasized the importance of taking charge of one's career. Books such as *Control Your Destiny or Someone Else Will* by Noel Tichy and Stratford Sherman,[27] and Harvard Business Review's *On Managing Yourself*[28] argue this important point.

The point is, the knowledge and technological skills individuals bring with them to the workplace are transportable and are not lost when they leave one organization and move to another.

To the employer this may feel like "reduced loyalty and commitment" but to the individual it feels like preservation, learning, and growth.

Increased Time Burdens. Years of downsizing, outsourcing and embracing "Lean" philosophies have created a "time famine." In essence, this is the common complaint much of the adult population of North America articulates as: "I don't have enough time!" And it is reflective of individuals feeling as though they have too much to do and too little time in which to do it. Sound familiar?

Flexible Work Arrangements are Not Keeping up with Employee Preferences. Although flexible work arrangements are not a new concept, my experience across many organizations has been that employees are required to show up for work physically; working remotely and with flexible schedules has not been the norm. In some cases, those with flex hours have limited freedom regarding when and where to work.

---

[27] Noel Tichy and Stratford Sherman, *Control your destiny or someone else will* (New York, Doubleday, 1994)

[28] Harvard Business Review, "On Managing Yourself," (Harvard Business School Publishing Corporation, Boston 2005)

The majority of employees have to commit to a specific day to work at home or a specific day to take off if they work a compressed work schedule. However that may have been in the past, it will be interesting to see how the 2020 Coronavirus pandemic affects alternative work arrangements going forward.

This is an exciting time to be on the work-life journey because so much is changing, and so much is possible. Regardless of where you are in your career journey you may find the following list of basic truths about the changing nature of work interesting. They stem from both my own experiences and the rich insights of others, and they may give you some new ways of approaching your future working life.

Truth #1

Work today is now more cognitively demanding and complex than ever. One of the primary reasons for this is the pace of change. In many workplaces, individuals are challenged to keep pace with rapidly changing technologies and processes. This trend is forecast to continue into the future.[29]

Truth #2

As poet John Donne famously said in the 17th Century, "No man is an island," and this certainly holds true in the context of workplaces. Today most work activities involve at least some level of a team-based approach in which members of the team contribute towards the final product or service.

Truth #3

More than ever before, individuals must be technologically savvy, and continue to expand their technological competence, if they want to stay relevant in the workplace.

---

[29] Kai-Fu Lee, *AI Super-Powers China, Silicon Valley and the New World Order* (Boston, Houghton Mifflin Harcourt, 2018)

Truth #4

Organizations and individuals which fail to stay abreast of changing technologies become obsolete much faster than those that do invest in keeping up to date.

Think about the retail industry and the number of large retail outlets that have filed for bankruptcy or simply closed. It's incredible to think how quickly that landscape has changed — forever.

In addition to risking becoming obsolete, when we fail to stay up-to-date and innovate with new technologies, we can also find ourselves working harder (or at least feeling as though we are), rather than working smarter.

Truth #5

One truth I hear repeatedly in my work with organizations is that there are more time pressures because of the demand for instant service, instant responses…instant everything.

Carrying mobile devices keeps us feeling connected 24/7 while feeding expectations of instant service.

Caution: there are psychological downsides to being connected 24/7—particularly the potential for cognitive overload, which contributes to burnout.

Truth #6

The rapidly expanding use of mobile technologies means the entire world has become our potential market. This has the potential to offer increased opportunities while at the same time it has expanded the competition for goods and services.

Next, we'll recap a few of the key trends we've seen and will continue to see – in our workplaces:

Recap of Key Points

1. There is a growing trend towards diverse and inclusive workplaces; research suggests diverse workplaces have many advantages over those that are more homogeneous. Diversity lends itself to opportunities for creativity and "out of the box" solutions.

2. Technology has changed our workplaces forever. The internet and smart phones are only a couple of the more recent innovations that have changed the landscape. More will follow!

3. We can expect the Millennial generation will predominate in our workplaces.

4. We can expect the use of technology, AI, and big data to increase, with significant impacts on the way work is done. Some jobs will be automated out of existence and others will be augmented or done differently.

5. Technology offers us an opportunity to eliminate mundane and repetitive work and replace it with more cognitively demanding work, which is both good and bad news. The good news: Work is likely to feel more challenging, which is essentially good for humans. The bad news is that too much challenging work can overload and overwhelm people and result in burnout.

6. Hand-in-hand with the trend towards "gigs" or short-term jobs and work activities is the acknowledgement that most people cannot—or should not—expect to have a job for life. Jobs, work, and careers are more dynamic and fluid than previously, which means there is likely to be less security.

7. Psychological Contract: There really is no such thing as "a job for life."

Creating Your Career / Denise O'Brien

Best Advice and Tips to Navigate the Changing Nature of Work and the Workplace

- Stay abreast of changing technology: Regardless of your age, or the point you might be at in your work and life journey, it is absolutely worth putting forth energy to stay abreast of technology.

  During my research, one woman shared with me that although she had retired from employment, she continued to take seminars on technology because she realizes "that so much of life happens on the computer." She took full advantage of the free seminars offered to seniors in her community. A wise woman indeed!

- Build a network of professionals: As pointed out in Chapter 1, regardless of the point you are at in your career path, I encourage you to join associations relevant to your profession. Take advantage of the programs, services, professional development, and networking opportunities offered by these associations in order to stay abreast of industry trends.

- Keep your CV up-to-date: The reality is that the "job for life" phenomenon is a thing of the past. There are no guarantees.

  I can't emphasize enough the importance of keeping your résumé current with your skills, competencies, experiences, successes, credentials etc…and take ownership of your work-life journey.

During my research one individual, whom I'll refer to as Todd, explained that the best boss he ever had was the one who encouraged him to always have his résumé ready for the next opportunity.

I asked Todd, "wasn't your manager concerned that you'd find another job, with another company?"

Todd's response was, "Sure. However, it was a risk he was willing to take. Better to be surrounded by individuals with an understanding of their value, than to manage a team with individuals that never take stock, because they become weak links on the team." This is such wise advice for Todd's manager to impart. (Todd left the organization for a more senior role with another company. He and his former manager remain good friends.)

- Burnout: As mentioned earlier in this chapter burnout is not something we choose. Rather, it happens when we feel the demands placed upon us are greater than the personal resources we have to deal with the demands.

- Pay attention to the symptoms of burnout and inform yourself about options for help. (There are lots of great tips offered at the end of each chapter in this book.

  Although the tips do not pertain strictly to burnout, all of the advice is offered by others who have successfully navigated their work-life, including burnout. Thus, you will find that many have applications to help with burnout, as well).

Chapter 3

Growth and Maintenance Phase

One of the biggest things I've learned is that I don't have to always be right.

—Jeffrey B. Swartz

This chapter includes a variety of topics related to career growth and maintenance I wish I'd been aware of—and understood—much earlier in my working life. Before I share advice on very important topics to help you maintain and grow in your work, let me put the importance of this chapter into context.

According to the results of a recent survey,[30] approximately 73% of Canadians feel some degree of stress at work. Interestingly, one of the top sources of stress at work is…people. These "people" might be our co-workers, the boss, our customers, patients, contractors, vendors, clients, etc.

The reality is that almost all work requires at least some degree of interaction with others. There is just no escaping the fact that to maintain and grow in our work we need to interact with people.

---

[30] Susan Crompton, "What's stressing the stressed? Main sources of stress among workers," *Statistics Canada*

The Importance of Emotional Intelligence

I referenced earlier the fact that the changing landscape of work has brought about an increased emphasis on social and emotional intelligence. Therefore, I thought it useful to provide more information about this highly important type of intelligence.

When I first heard the language of "emotional intelligence," I must admit I was skeptical. Even worse, I was asked to study and become certified in administering emotional intelligence programs to others. I approached the study of emotional intelligence with a cynical view of what it might offer. However, I gradually came to the realization that emotional intelligence—which is essentially the capacity to manage our emotions, moment by moment, regardless of the circumstances—is one of the greatest assets we can leverage in our work and personal lives. Let me repeat this: emotional intelligence is one of the greatest assets we can leverage.

Emotional intelligence is a term first used by Peter Salovey and Jack Mayer [31] to describe "the ability to perceive emotions, to access and generate emotions so as to assist thought, to understand emotions and emotional meanings, and to reflectively regulate emotions in ways which promote emotional and intellectual growth."

In other words, emotional intelligence is simply "street smarts" that allows us to be able to read the landscape and intuitively grasp the appropriate emotional response in any given situation. It's about remaining unflustered when confronted with stressful situations. It's about being engaged and maintaining a "glass half-full attitude," rather than adopting a "glass half-empty" perspective.

---

[31] Steven Stein and Howard Book, *The EQ Edge: Emotional Intelligence and Your Success* (Jossy-Bass 2011, San Francisco)

Creating Your Career / Denise O'Brien

As I have facilitated workshops on emotional intelligence, I have often heard comments such as,

"I don't buy this stuff."

"It's all about being touchy-feely at work."

"I wish people would keep their feelings and emotions to themselves rather than bringing them to work."

In reality, emotions and feelings are everywhere in our workplace, and dealing with them at work is unavoidable. Emotions are hardwired into us and they influence our thinking, which affects the choices we make in our behaviour. Feelings and emotions lack logic and are not objective. Feelings aren't right or wrong. We are free to feel whichever way we want—however, we need to be aware that feelings and emotions can be one of our biggest de-railers at work.

This is not because displaying emotions at work is inappropriate or unwelcome. Rather, emotions can become a problem when the level of emotion is not perceived to be reasonable or congruent to the circumstances. For instance, say that on the drive to work you were cut off by another driver and you felt angry and frustrated. As you arrive at work and are getting out of your vehicle, you spill your coffee down the front of your new jacket. Grrrr ... Even before you enter the workplace you may be feeling ready to take your feelings out on the first person who speaks to you.

For example: maybe you yell at a co-worker because she asked you where she could find paper for the photocopier. Or you slammed a door because you felt upset with your manager. Other emotional displays such as loud sighs, eye-rolling and crossing one's arms defensively may come across as anger. Trust me, these behaviours will not serve you well at work.

On the other hand, if you have a highly developed level of emotional intelligence, you are likely able to regulate your emotions and you will not take out your frustrations on your colleagues.

Here are a few practical examples of how emotions have derailed individuals at work:

1. John is in his mid-40s. He is a hardworking individual who runs his own business, which he purchased 15-years ago from his former boss. John has succeeded in growing the business in a highly competitive market. Over time, John has also expanded the number of people he employs. Increasingly, John feels a greater level of pressure to bring in more business because he knows his employees are counting on him for their livelihoods.

   Unfortunately, because of everything John has on his plate, he is short-tempered at work and comes across as moody, quick to anger and generally unapproachable. As a result, he has a difficult time retaining staff, which leaves him constantly scrambling to hire replacements to meet customer demands. John regards his employees as the problem. He views them as lazy, too sensitive, and not loyal to him and his company.

2. Sue works as a Customer Service Representative. She has been with the organization for almost 25-years. Sue regards herself as having a greater level of knowledge and expertise than anyone else in her department. She feels frustrated and resentful that her manager does not see her potential. At times, Sue has said she feels "everyone else is given opportunities but since I'm not the manager's favourite I don't get them. It is so unfair. I always get the short-end of the stick."

3. Jerry is married with three teenage children. He is good at his job and comfortably settled in his organization. Over the last three or four months, Jerry has noticed that his co-worker, Jason, has made some disparaging remarks about the quality of his work. For example, one day in the lunchroom Jason made a snide comment about a deadline Jerry had missed. He seemed to be taking great enjoyment from pointing out that Jerry didn't seem to be able "to keep up because of his age." Jerry now feels so uncomfortable interacting with Jason that he feels himself visibly shaking when he sees him coming towards him in the hallway.

Imagine working with John or Sue or Jason. These would not be easy people to work with. The reality is we all have a bit of John, Sue and even Jason in us at times …we're all human.

Emotional Intelligence in a Nutshell

As human beings we all take our emotions and feelings everywhere we go, including into every conversation and interaction we have with people. We bring our happiness, excitement, enthusiasm, and laughter—as well as our frustration, disappointment, anger, sadness, and worry.

Workplace actions lead to many different emotional responses. Even without meaning to, we can (and do) offend, hurt, and frustrate our colleagues.

Leaders and managers can hurt employees' feelings through insensitive attitudes and decision-making, unreasonable expectations, inflexible practices and policies, and poorly managed change. Inevitably, personal situations also lead to emotional responses in the workplace.

Personal lives are messier, and home and work/life are bleeding together more these days than ever before, as we all think about and deal with difficult personal situations at work—including divorces, marital problems, family health issues, financial problems, issues with children, and elder care.

Additionally, some of us simply take things very personally. Others may be highly emotionally invested in their work, personally connected to it, and extremely sensitive to anything that comes across as criticism.

The truth is that emotions are normal, healthy responses to stimuli in our environments.

Emotions help keep us safe from harm. For example, if a fire alarm goes off, I am alerted to the potential harm of a fire. It triggers a feeling of fear which prompts me to get out of the building and out of harm's way.

On the other hand, as described in the scenarios of John, Sue and Jason, our emotional responses sometimes do not serve us well.

Often, we are responding in ways that are default emotional responses; we let our emotions manage us, rather than the other way around.

For example, Jerry's response to simply observing Jason was to respond with anxiety and fear. Is the emotional response appropriate to the circumstances? How is that response serving Jerry and his professional, working relationship with Jason?

The bottom line is that our emotional responses can significantly de-rail us. Learning to notice our emotions is an important first step.

There are many good resources to help us understand our emotional intelligence. I've included a short questionnaire here to help you get started thinking about how well you might be managing your emotions at work.

Creating Your Career / Denise O'Brien

Emotional Intelligence Questionnaire

The emotional intelligence questionnaire below provides a straightforward way of helping to self-assess Emotional Intelligence – and it measures three key dimensions:

1. **Attention:** I'm able to express feelings appropriately
2. **Awareness:** I understand how I'm feeling
3. **Regulation:** I can regulate emotional states correctly

20 Questions to Assess Your Emotional Intelligence

Please read the following statements about your emotions and feelings and indicate your degree of agreement or disagreement. Please circle the number for each answer that most closely "sounds like" your preference. Don't spend too much time on each item. Be honest! All answers are good.

---

1. I pay close attention to my feelings. 1 2 3 4 5
2. I don't usually worry about what I feel. 1 2 3 4 5
3. I usually spend time thinking about my emotions. 1 2 3 4 5
4. I feel it's important to pay attention to my emotions. 1 2 3 4 5
5. I try not to let my feelings affect my thoughts. 1 2 3 4 5
6. I am tuned into my mood. 1 2 3 4 5
7. I pay close attention to other's feelings. 1 2 3 4 5
8. I am good at reading other people's feelings. 1 2 3 4 5
9. I almost always know how I feel. 1 2 3 4 5
10. I usually know how others may be feeling. 1 2 3 4 5
11. I often notice my feelings in different situations. 1 2 3 4 5
12. I am comfortable discussing my feelings. 1 2 3 4 5
13. Sometimes I can say what my emotions are. 1 2 3 4 5
14. I can understand my feelings. 1 2 3 4 5
15. I usually have a positive outlook. 1 2 3 4 5
16. I know what triggers negative emotions in me. 1 2 3 4 5
17. I have a "glass half full" attitude about most things. 1 2 3 4 5
18. I try to think positive thoughts. 1 2 3 4 5
19. When things go wrong, I'm quickly able to let go of my frustrations and change my mood. 1 2 3 4 5
20. I work hard at maintaining a positive outlook. 1 2 3 4 5

Total: _____

Results: Add up your score to rank your Emotional Intelligence. Your results will give you a good idea of your opportunity in the given area:
85 – 100: Nailed it! Keep up the good work.
55 – 84: You're likely doing okay and with added effort you can nail it!
0 – 54: Some work to do – but not to worry. You've got this!

Navigating Relationships

Another critical aspect of work we need to be wary of as we navigate the career journey lies in the area of the effective management of workplace relationships. There are at least five important ones which will require our attention:

- The relationship we have with our boss or manager
- Our relationships with peers and co-workers
- The relationship we have with the organization
- Our relationships with professional networks and other associations
- Our personal and family relationships and the way in which these impact upon our work

Our Relationship with the Boss

The relationship you have with your boss can be career-building or career-ending. What's your pleasure?

Research has consistently demonstrated that the number one reason people leave their job is because they cannot stand working with their boss.

If you're having relationship challenges with your manager, I strongly recommend you figure out what you can do to help make the relationship better. Here are five suggestions to help you get started:

1. **Let the work first start with you.**

    If you want or need to improve the relationship you share with your boss, the first place to start is with yourself. In other words, there are likely things you are doing — or perhaps not doing—that are contributing to the state of the relationship. Thus, if you are spending a lot of time blaming your boss, and finding fault with him or her, you are likely a big part of the problem.

I know this is not what you want to hear, nor is it what you likely believe to be true. However, I speak from personal experience and the many conversations I have had with others over the years. Thinking negatively about our boss affects how we come across.

Example:

Jenna is a bright, highly educated, no-nonsense woman. She has worked with ABC Company for more than 20 years and has always received positive feedback on her performance.

Jenna's colleagues see her as hardworking and focused on getting things done, rather than as a socializer who builds relationships. She really doesn't seem to have a lot in common with her colleagues, although perhaps she hasn't taken the time to get to know them.

Jenna had aspirations to be the Division Superintendent overseeing the work of the five units within the division. Just about the time she saw herself as ready to move into the Division Superintendent role, the organization re-structured and without warning the position was eliminated.

Jenna was shocked, angry, and frustrated and she felt as though she had been stabbed in the back by the organization and, in particular, by her boss. She brought her negative feelings with her to every conversation and interaction with colleagues. She became quick to anger, and she was quite unpredictable. Her colleagues felt as though they were walking on eggshells and were concerned they might set her off at any moment.

To make a long story short, Jenna's negativity got in the way of her having a productive relationship with her boss. She mostly arrived at work angry, and things did not improve throughout the day. Her boss was initially understanding of Jenna's deep sense of disappointment at not getting the Division Superintendent position.

However, as time went on, she became frustrated and disappointed in Jenna's behaviour. She came to realize that Jenna was a negative influence in the workplace and disciplinary action was taken.

2. Keep the lines of communication open.

Work hard at nurturing a respectful, cooperative professional relationship with your boss. In your communications with him or her, be open-minded, ask questions, check the facts, avoid assumptions and do your best to follow the rules.

In my work, I often hear people say, "communication is one of the biggest problems in our organization." The reality is, communication is rarely the cause of the problem. Rather, in our workplaces we frequently make assumptions which may or may not be accurate and which lead us to think, feel, and behave in certain ways.

All of these things contribute to misunderstandings and confusion, which affect the way we communicate with each other. Take extra effort to develop effective communication with your boss.

3. **Seek feedback.**

   One of the simplest ways to figure out how to work better with your boss is to ask for feedback via questions such as:

   - What can I do differently to work better with you?

   - How do you prefer to receive information, i.e. email messages, face-to-face meetings, etc.?

   - What else can I do to help support the unit?

   - Do you have suggestions for improvement?

4. **Offer to help.**

   Look for opportunities to offer to help with work-related tasks and activities. Rather than being difficult to work with, look for ways to make things better. Offer suggestions and provide constructive feedback to be helpful. As I write this book, workplaces are struggling to deal with the fallout of the COVID-19 pandemic.

   A senior manager recently shared with me that during this difficult time she has been so touched by one member of her team who continually offers to help out wherever and whenever she can.

   While most members of her team look to this senior manager to be the "knower-of-all-things" to allay their fears during a turbulent time, one member of her team has stood out as someone who can be depended upon during a difficult time.

Her offers of assistance, without grumbling and complaining, make her standout from the rest. (Interestingly, the senior manager hasn't needed this individual to take on anything extra but just the offer has made a difference.)

5. Be positive and optimistic.

Positive, optimistic individuals are much easier to like. If you want to be respected, while building a harmonious relationship with your boss, approach work with an optimistic and solution-focused mindset. Stop grumbling and complaining about… everything.

If you have a legitimate concern about something, speak to your boss about it. Accept his or her answer, even if it is not the one you wanted to hear, and then let it go.

Recall the example of Jenna: she became her own worst enemy (and her boss's) because she could not release her anger over what soon became an old issue.

Our Relationships with Peers and Co-Workers

Research indicates[32] that when we have a friend at work, or at least we enjoy working with our co-workers, we are more likely to enjoy going to work, and we are less likely to want to leave the organization. According to statistics,[33] the average adult spends approximately 35% of his or her life at work.

---

[32] AnnaMarie Mann, "Why we need best friends at work," *Gallup Workplace*

[33] Andrew Naber, "One third of your life is spent at work," *Gettysburg College*

Broken down even further, the average adult may spend an estimated 90,000 hours of life at work. Wow! Imagine spending that much time with people who you don't get along with well.

In the previous section I outlined five ways we can strengthen the relationship we share with our boss. Those suggestions work with all of our workplace relationships.

In addition to those ones, I offer a few others to help maintain effective relationships with co-workers:

1. **Manage your emotions**

    You will not be a "favourite" if you come to work and take out your frustrations on the people around you.

    Take responsibility for your emotions and be conscientious enough to express the right emotion in the right way and at the right time. (This might be a good time to review the section on Emotional Intelligence again.)

2. **Do not engage in gossip.**

    I believe there's really no positive outcome to gossip in the workplace. Research[34] suggests gossiping is a social activity that has been with us a long time – and will likely be an activity we will not get rid of anytime soon.

    Gossip in the workplace is a time waster, it ruins morale, and it can spread faster than a bad cold.

---

[34]Bianca Beersma and Geren VanKleef, "Why People Gossip: An Empirical Analysis of Social Motives, Antecedents, and Consequences," *Journal of Applied Social Psychology*, pp. 2640-2670, 2012

If you perceive gossip is a problem in your workplace, what should you do? You will not be able to change the culture overnight, but you can change your own choices and behaviours to make a positive difference. Here are some practical tips:

- **Observe:** Before launching yourself into office politics, observe. See how people relate and learn the unofficial roles certain individuals in your workplace have adopted.

    If you notice one person who consistently makes trouble, have as little interaction with that person as possible.

- **Be busy:** Gossipmongers want attention. If you're delving into your work, you can't be available to appreciate their latest tales.

- **Don't participate:** If there is gossip at your place of work, let it stop with you. If someone passes a "juicy story" on to you, don't pass it any further. Take personal responsibility to act with integrity.

- **Turn it around**: Inject positivity into the situation. It isn't nearly as much fun to spread negative news if it's spoiled by a complimentary phrase about the person under attack.

- **Keep your private life private:** Don't trust personal information with coworkers. Remember, if they are gossiping about others, they will gossip about you, too. Don't give them ammunition.

- **Choose your friends wisely at work:** You spend a lot of time at work: the average adult spends approximately one-third of their life at work. It's quite natural for friendships to develop. Share information sparingly until you are sure you have created a high level of trust.

- **Behave appropriately at work:** Remember that work is not the place to share all types of information.

- **Be courageous:** You know you are morally correct by not gossiping. So does the one spreading the gossip. If you confront that person and confidently tell him or her that such behaviour is making it uncomfortable for you and other coworkers, it's likely to stop.

- Keep in mind, it takes a lot of courage to speak up to the person spreading the gossip or speaking negatively about someone. Be courageous.

- **Talk to your manager:** Gossiping wastes a lot of company time and it hurts morale. A company interested in a healthy work environment will value the opportunity to correct this type of situation.

- Keep in mind that gossiping to your manager about the "gossip" can make the problem bigger if you don't handle it well.

Keep the conversation grounded in the facts, as you know them. Avoid embellishments and be upfront about any assumptions you might be making about the "gossip." Once you have brought it to your manager's attention – leave it alone.

3. **Be a team player.**

   In Chapter 2 I stressed that the team is the building block of most organizational structures.

   In fact, most workplaces have some form of a teamwork structure which involves *interdependency* for completing work and accomplishing goals.

   If you are just starting out on your career journey it is highly probable you will be working in an organization as a member of a team.

   Even if you own the company, you are likely to have others working with you on your team. Being a team player is an important competency.

   Here is a list of suggestions to help develop your capacity to be a strong team player:

   - **Do your job**: Know what you are expected to be doing at work and do it…to the absolute best of your ability. If you do not know how to do parts of it, ask for help.

   - **Be conscientious:** Be dependable, diligent, and someone who can be trusted to follow through on your commitments and promises.

   - **Offer to help others**: Look for opportunities to offer to help others. It may not require much effort, or take much time, but offers of assistance make a significant difference in the workplace.

Be someone who willingly jumps into action to help a colleague. Be the colleague who does a "good deed" without looking for anything in return.

- **Give credit where credit is due**: Do not take credit for work completed by other people. If someone acknowledges you for something you did not do, let them know the credit belongs to your co-worker.

  Go out of your way to acknowledge your colleagues to others. Speaking highly of colleagues reflects back on you.

- **Be appreciative:** Let your colleagues know when they have done something well. Give them kudos and positive feedback. Make your appreciation timely and frequent.
-
  My good friend, Sarah McVanel, is a leading expert on the importance of appreciation and recognition at work.

  In her book, *Forever Recognize Others' Greatness*, [35]Sarah and her co-author, Brenda Zalter-Minden, note that in our workplaces, people are hungry for appreciation.

---

[35] Sarah McVanel and Brenda Zalter-Minden, Forever recognize others' greatness: Solution-focused strategies for satisfied staff, high-performing teams, and healthy bottom lines, (Toronto, BPS Books, 2015)

She offers a plethora of tips and suggestions for how to work better together by simply learning to "recognize others' greatness."

- **Be a good listener:** Learn to be a good listener because good listeners are often in short supply.

  A good listener asks thoughtful questions, displays genuine interest, and allows you time to respond.

  And a good listener is someone who does not reveal a confidence or repeat something they have been told.

  In my experience, listening to understand is one of the most important aspects of communication. If you do nothing else to develop your communication skills, learn to be a good listener. This quality will serve you well.

- **Apologize:** Take responsibility for mistakes and apologize. Let go of the mistakes of others and choose to work cooperatively. Grudges are heavy loads to carry.

- **Be upfront in your communication:** Be someone who says what they mean and means what they say.

- This behaviour is a reflection of your character. Be honourable and courageous in your communication.

Our Relationship with the Organization

The relationship we have with the organization is another important relationship that will have significant ramifications for our work and career.

I must admit I was more than mid-way along my career journey before I ever gave any consideration to the organization in relation to my career.

Essentially, this relationship involves asking ourselves "what have I done this year, this month, this week, and today to contribute to the organization's mission and priorities?"

Too often we get caught up in thinking about our work in terms of getting the tasks-at-hand done in the present moment. We may not give much thought to how our work is contributing to—and is interconnected with—the overall goals and work of the organization.

It is important to recognize our work is interconnected with the work of others and that collectively we all have a part to play in the organization's success.

Make it your weekly practice to ask yourself the following questions:

- What have I specifically done this week to contribute to my organization?

- How have I demonstrated my commitment to the organization's success?

- What one thing can I do this week to contribute to my organization's success?

If you ask yourself these questions and you feel uncertain about how to answer because you have no idea how your work is making a difference or contributing towards organizational success, I offer the following advice:

- Seek feedback from your manager to ensure you're on the right path and contributing in ways that are making a difference.

- Notice what others are doing and model those who are getting positive feedback.

Our Relationship with Professional Networks and Associations

I cannot over-emphasize the importance of nurturing effective relationships with professional networks and associations. I was part way along in my career when an acquaintance suggested I join the local human resources professional association. Although I was not working in human resources at the time, the acquaintance knew it was a career move I had been considering. I took her advice and joined the association; I am deeply grateful for the advice.

By joining the association I gained access to information about professional trends, career and educational opportunities, credentialing requirements and, most importantly, access to human resources professionals… the same human resources professionals responsible for recruitment and selection – or, more simply put, hiring. Another very practical benefit of joining a professional association is that it affords opportunities to be exposed to the terminology of your field, supporting you to become more fluent in the "lingo" of the profession.

This advice is valuable for everybody, regardless of where you are on your career journey. If you are a student just starting out, know that many associations offer student membership rates. Some professional associations have restrictions about membership and will allow only fully qualified individuals to become members.

There may be opportunities to attend as a guest, however. Take advantage of all your professional association offers, such as conferences, seminars, trade shows, or speaking events. These are wonderful opportunities to expand your knowledge and grow your network.

Personal and Family Relationships

Although this book is primarily focused on one's career in the changing landscape of work, I am a strong proponent of the importance of balance; it's critical to demonstrate balance in the time and energy we dedicate to our professional and personal lives.

In other words, do not put so much time and energy into your work that there is nothing left for your personal and family relationships.

If you follow the advice I have already offered to effectively navigate the relationships with your boss, co-workers, the organization and professional associations, then this section will likely be fairly easy for you.

Managing relationships is about knowing and choosing one's priorities. I encourage you to be wise about your choices. Do not put work ahead of relationships with those you love, or with whom you enjoy spending time.

While researching to write this book one individual put it this way: "one of my biggest regrets is that I worked so many hours that I missed time with my children. It also put a strain on the marriage and eventually we drifted apart."

Elements that Feed Us at Work

At some point in your career journey you are inevitably going to be contemplating, "what's next for me?"

I invite you to consider the work you are doing already and ask yourself these questions.

- Do you enjoy your work?
- What parts of your work do you enjoy the most?
- How satisfied do you feel doing your work?
- Do you have a Job or a Career? (recall the different meanings of these terms from Chapter 1)
- What else would you like to achieve in your work?

During my research I actually posed these questions to others. Below are some of the responses I heard about the best parts of work. As you read the list, reflect on how you answered the questions. Do you see yourself reflected in the responses? The best part of my work is:

- "Helping others"
- "Making an impact"
- "Autonomy"
- "Being acknowledged for contribution and accomplishment"
- "Interacting with others"
- "Feeling like I'm valued for what I'm producing"

- "Opportunities for learning and development"
- "Creativity and individual expression"

Notice the connection to relationships and the impact they have upon how we feel about our work.

The diagram below illustrates the interdependent nature of our relationships at work.

Put effort into nurturing effective, healthy relationships.

I am confident it will impact your work life in very positive ways.

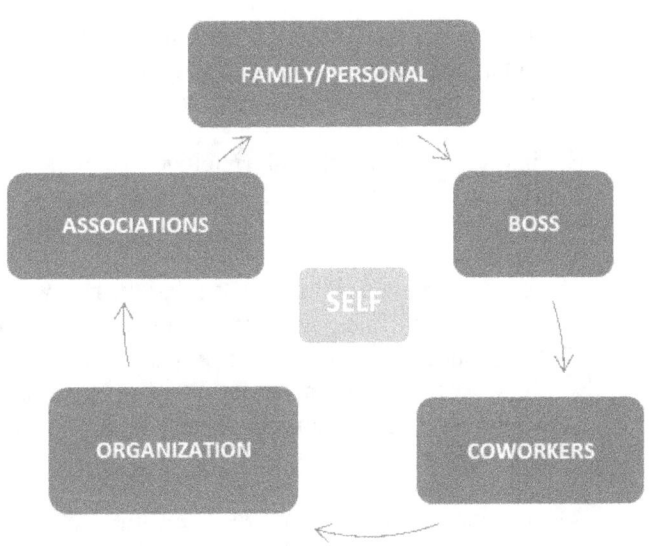

Recap of Key Points

1. According to researchers, most of us feel some degree of stress at work and often the primary source of our stress is other people. It seems reasonable, then, that learning how to navigate "people" matters at work is of critical importance.

2. Emotional intelligence is one of the greatest assets we can leverage at work.

   There are many resources to help develop our emotional intelligence. I encourage you to continue to learn whatever you can in this regard.

3. Having a low emotional intelligence will be a significant career de-railer. Learn how to manage your emotions.

4. There are at least five important relationships we have with our work which will impact upon our success. These include the ones we have with our boss, co-workers, the organization, our professional associations and networks, and our personal relationships.

   All of these relationships require time, effort and attention. Learn to balance them.

Best Advice and Tips to Navigate Career Growth and Maintenance

- **Pick your battles**. Don't waste energy fighting about unimportant issues. Not everything is worth fighting over.

- **Accept you cannot control everything**: take responsibility for that which you are responsible for, and accept that not everything is within your control.

- **Flexibility and adaptability** are competencies which will serve you well because change is constant. Be courageous.

- **Be open-minded**: Approach everything with an open-mind.

- **Be respectful and courteous**: These qualities are always in style.

- **Learn continuously**: Take advantage of co-op programs, internships, etc. All situations are opportunities for learning.

- **Work hard and take "crappy jobs."** They contribute to your growth.

- **Accept that at times life will be hard**: Get over it.

- **Practice gratitude**: those who show appreciation to others are much easier to like. They tend to attract other positive people. Stop complaining about what you don't have or what you feel isn't fair. Count your blessings. Appreciate others.

Creating Your Career / Denise O'Brien

Chapter 4

Complacency

> **The enemy of the best is the good.**
>
> **—Voltaire**

So, you secured work and you have settled in well. Perhaps you remained in the original position you were hired to fill, or maybe you have changed positions. It's possible you took the work as a "job" and a "means to an end," rather than work you aspired to be doing for the rest of your career...but for whatever reason, you are now feeling disengaged, and maybe even a little discouraged. You are not feeling energetic or passionate about going to work.

Maybe you show up at work and go through the motions of being productive but, in reality, you are in the building in body only, while your head and heart are elsewhere. Too many people put in face time. They show up for work, and think that is good enough. Many people even like to believe they are working hard. Most believe—or at least like to believe—they are contributing.

For many people work is no longer a source of great pride and the "bloom is off the rose." Even when they put in a lot of time, they do not accomplish much. They do not add a lot of value. They do not feel good about it. And it robs them of dignity and feeds complacency and what I refer to as a "victim mentality."

Here's an example:

Richard is 37 years old, and he is married with three young children. He earned a college diploma and then went to work in the public service in a junior management role.

He is bright, honest, and believes in doing an honest day's work for an honest day's pay. He works in a unionized organization which means all work, including roles and responsibilities, wages, and vacations, etc. are governed by a collective agreement.

His organization is publicly funded and hierarchal: there are many levels of management and decisions tend to be made at the more senior levels.

Over time, Richard has become somewhat cynical about work. He has come to believe his employer really only needs him to show up physically; he feels there is no real expectation that he needs to do much to receive his wages, as they are deposited into his account automatically bi-weekly.

Richard realizes he is being paid regardless of his output and he has begun to feel as though he has absolutely no way to change things. In fact, when he told his manager he would like more work to do he was told, "No. The collective agreement requires me to assign work to another person."

Thus, Richard has become complacent. He shows up to work and does what he is told, or what is expected of him. Although he had the potential to be a star performer Richard settles into a habit of mediocre performance.

Richard's story is a good example of how employers unwittingly perpetuate complacency by their failure to hold people accountable to doing good work. This is most unfortunate because as humans we are driven to want to make a difference, to contribute, to fit in, and to do our part in society and at work.

What Feeds Complacency?

I believe a complacent employee is an individual who feels a sense of entitlement. Dr. Judith Bardwick[36] says entitlement denotes a belief one does not have to *earn* what one receives. People with this belief have come to believe that they are owed, that they are entitled. They are owed because of who they are, not because of what they contribute. They receive because it is their "due." It is their right. If they were denied what they expected, it would be "unfair." Does this language and way of thinking sound familiar?

There are many downsides to complacency. Here are a few to illustrate the point:

Complacency destroys motivation. It robs us of the satisfaction of earning what we receive because we feel like everything is "owed" to us. As we sit back and wait for everything to come to us without work or effort, we lose our ability to achieve on our merit.

Deep down inside, we do not feel good about this situation and over time it crushes our self-esteem. Some argue this is a "generational issue." I disagree. Complacency afflicts all ages.

---

[36] Judith Bardwick, "Danger in the Comfort Zone: From Boardroom to Mailroom – How to Break the Entitlement Habit That's Killing American Business," *American Management Association*, 1991

Reward without effort feels dishonest. It makes people feel like frauds and imposters. For example, when we get raises, bonuses, and other benefits pretty much as a matter of course, our incentive to work erodes. And reward without much effort feeds complacency.

Complacency breeds fear. More and more people have become paralyzed by the threat of layoffs and organizational uncertainty and this makes them focus on protecting their jobs rather than doing them. The fear of job loss does not necessarily incite individuals to work harder, or secure other employment.

It often ignites feelings of anger, resentment and hopelessness instead. Fear makes us victims. It does not inspire, motivate or energize. Do not become a victim of your own fear.

People are energized by challenge and growth. When we know our work will be judged and rewards will be based on accomplishment, we feel challenged to learn and grow. We feel motivated to work hard to achieve. We don't feel complacent; we feel worthy and purposeful. And we move away from complacency.

The Root of Complacency

I regard complacency as a legacy of years of affluence. In the postwar decades, organizations began to grant job security without regard to how well people performed or how much they contributed. The industrial era brought about the production of more products and services which ultimately fed consumer demand. Government infrastructures, programs, and services expanded to support changing societal needs.

The bottom line: there was a lot of work to be done and workplaces struggled to find enough employees to allow them to keep pace with consumer demand. We've all heard stories from parents or elderly family members about people who dropped out of high school to take a job, earning their position immediately, and with little or no competition.

Since the mid-to-late 1980s and beyond, however, organizations have come to realize that at times there are employees who are "playing at working." Some, like Richard in our earlier example, are busy looking busy.

And because no one in the organization has said, "That won't do," they have, in effect, been saying "that's fine." Over time, complacency has become so systemically entrenched we no longer even recognize it. We assume we are entitled to that which we receive, and more.

Diagnosing Complacency

To learn whether you might be suffering from complacency, or are perhaps on the road to complacency, I invite you complete the following quiz on the next page:

Review each statement and rank your response by circling a corresponding number. Numbers are ranked from 1 (not at all) through 10 (absolutely). For example, "I feel engaged at work" – rank the level of your engagement with a number between 1 – 10 in the Rank column. Be honest. This information is for your eyes only.

COMPLACENCY QUIZ											
	Not at all									Absolutely!	Rank
I feel engaged at work	1	2	3	4	5	6	7	8	9	10	
I rarely find myself completing tasks without thought	1	2	3	4	5	6	7	8	9	10	
I show initiative at work	1	2	3	4	5	6	7	8	9	10	
I take courses to continue to grow and develop	1	2	3	4	5	6	7	8	9	10	
I set personal and work goals	1	2	3	4	5	6	7	8	9	10	
I feel like I make a difference at work	1	2	3	4	5	6	7	8	9	10	

Creating Your Career / Denise O'Brien

I feel passionate about my work	1	2	3	4	5	6	7	8	9	10	
I feel optimistic	1	2	3	4	5	6	7	8	9	10	
I am treated fairly at work	1	2	3	4	5	6	7	8	9	10	
Things at work are mostly within my control	1	2	3	4	5	6	7	8	9	10	

Results:

Once you've completed the quiz add up your total marks. It should be fairly obvious from your results whether you may be a risk of being complacent. I would interpret your results as follows:

80 – 100: Safe Range - Navigating away from Complacency

55 – 79: Exercise Caution - Complacency up ahead

0 – 55: Warning – you may be stuck in Complacency

How Does Complacency Destroy Productivity?

1. It Institutionalizes Security

Informal tenure for everyone in an organization means keeping your position has nothing to do with the meaningful contributions you make.

Instead, you know you will likely keep your job simply because you have been around for a long time.

Here's an example of how informal tenure practices breed complacency:

> Dale is a maintenance manager working within the public sector. His job involves overseeing the maintenance of a large building and its surrounding property.
>
> One day, Dale's boss learned he had hired a contractor to do some maintenance work at the property in exchange for some "free of charge" work at Dale's home.
>
> An investigation confirmed Dale had breached trust and used his position to secure free services from the contractor. Dale's employer was reluctant to penalize Dale for his conduct because he was a long-service employee who had been around for many years.

Poorly designed or poorly understood performance management systems are also problematic. Many organizations regard performance management as a waste of time.

Some managers "go through the motions" and complete performance appraisals to appease their Human Resources Department but they see little-to-no-value in the process.

One manager noted that: "they don't really expect people to excel, so evaluating performance is a half-hearted exercise at best."

I agree. Poorly designed performance management systems are a waste of time and money.

On the other hand, I think it is critical that workplaces establish clear work goals with employees, provide honest, timely feedback on their progress, and support personal growth and development – all of which requires an effective performance management process.

The point is, performance management is beneficial. A faulty process is a waste of time and will undermine the workplace, rather than improve it.

The solution is to fix the process, not eliminate it.

A promotion system that doesn't reflect individual merit breeds mediocrity and complacency, and is indicative of a system that has institutionalized security.

An emphasis on precedent and a mentality of "this is how we've always done it" are also symptomatic of institutionalized security in an organization.

A compensation system that does not reflect what people do is problematic, especially if no one seems to know how to make it better. Human Resources personnel are often reluctant to revisit the compensation system because of the work implications and they know "you can't make everyone happy so let's just leave things as they are."

Maintaining the status quo breeds complacency.

These issues also contribute to complacency:

Committees with no real purpose or authority. Oh my gosh! One of the biggest time wasters at work (and in life) can be committees with no real purpose or authority. We often show up for committee meetings without an agenda or purpose.

Even if you have an agenda, is it absolutely necessary to meet in person, or can the information be shared in some other way, e.g. via email or internal internet post, or a conference call? Complacent employees show up and offer very little. They go through the motions.

Reward for years of service rather than actual service – I must admit this is one of my biggest pet peeves because I know it mostly hurts the organization rather than helps it.

The idea of service awards began in the 1940s after World War II with the rise of the industrial revolution and the subsequent boom economy.

Back then, companies such as General Electric started to reward loyal employees with long service awards such as gold watches, pins etc. It was a way of honoring employees for remaining loyal to a company despite other opportunities being available to them.

Fuelled largely by companies that marketed and sold service award paraphernalia, the idea of honoring long service with a trinket over time morphed into recognizing employees at all other service milestones as well. For example, some organizations now recognize service milestones of six months, one year, five years, etc.

In other words, organizations began organizing annual service award celebrations to recognize "service," rather than actual contribution. These formal recognition programs are a complete waste of time and money. They feed a mentality of entitlement and complacency.

These practices are harmful to workplaces because they fracture trust. Those in positions of power and authority have a responsibility to be role models for others. A mentality of "do as I say and not as I do" breeds confusion, distrust, and complacency.

Talk about pushing power down with no real empowerment or delegation: Actions speak much louder than words. For example, workplaces which rest decision-making authority at the top —or close to the top—of the organizational hierarchy leave those further down the hierarchal chain feeling less invested in the outcome. They shrug their shoulders and sit back to wait for decisions to be made.

2. Complacency Generates a Layer of Administrators Responsible for Making Sure No Mistakes are Made

Rules, Bureaucracy, and Hierarchy: Organizations with lots of rules usually have lots of checkers to make sure the rules are being obeyed. Institutions with too much job-related security thus tend to become more and more bureaucratic.

They add layers of rules to ensure mistakes are never made and they add layers of people to ensure the rules are explained, understood, updated and followed. Those engaged in bureaucracy often regard their work as urgent and important – regardless of whether or not it is.

Plenty of policies: One sure-fire way to know if your organization is complacent is if you are busy creating policies. If you have a policy for everything then, trust me, you are in trouble! Policies are about policing. It takes time to create and update them. And even more time to enforce them.

Don't get me wrong.

All workplaces require some policies—such as those relating to health and safety—in order to be compliant with provincial and federal laws. These policies serve a necessary purpose. On the other hand, many organizations go overboard and try to create policies for every possible contingency. That is not an achievable goal.

Lots and lots of paper. In complacent organizations, many people are busy covering their backsides. Emails, reports, etc. are printed and filed. In addition to lots and lots of paper, there are lots and lots of meetings. Is any of this sounding familiar? Believe me, if the bulk of your day is spent in meetings, you are on the path to complacency.

Meetings are about talking and planning to get things done. They do not actually get things done. When someone spends much of their time talking about doing things, they inevitably become someone who grumbles, "I am so busy! I don't have enough time to get things done!"

Do not get me wrong, it is important to have conversations with colleagues and to plan and coordinate work activities. However, be mindful of the amount of time you are spending in meetings generating plans and paperwork.

Pseudowork: In complacent organizations people concentrate on what looks good. Looking good is more important than doing good. Over time, form supplants substance. When complacency permeates the workplace, the appearance of being busy can equate in value to actually being busy.

Going through the motions, people are mostly unaware of how their work connects to the bottom line of the business. They feel busy but their efforts may not be contributing much. Thus, they are compensated for simply putting in time. Pseudowork diminishes our self-esteem. It is frustrating work. It breeds complacency.

3. Complacency Diminishes Integrity and Self-Worth

Passivity: In hierarchical organizations, where power comes from the top down, people look up and wait for orders. They pay close attention to the nuances of behaviour from those with more power. They know there is an unwritten contract which says "if you behave, you'll be okay.

No wonder people pay so much attention to knowing the rules, following the boss's lead, knowing the right people, and never looking like they make errors. All of this comes at the cost of risk-taking and innovating.

Hierarchical organizations feed passivity in people. But even as they resent being treated like children, and being given rules to follow, people are ambivalent. Rules give us an easy way to master situations. Rules give us security and protect us from having to think and make judgments.

In some situations we do follow the "unwritten rules" even though we don't always feel good about doing so.

I am reminded of the movie, *A Few Good Men,* as a perfect example of following unwritten organizational rules, even though the personal toll is high. In this movie a character named Daniel Kaffee (played by actor Tom Cruise) is a military lawyer defending two U.S. Marines who have been charged with killing a fellow Marine at the Guantanamo Bay Naval Base in Cuba.

Although Kaffee is known for seeking plea bargains, a fellow lawyer, Lieutenant Commander JoAnne Galloway (played by actress Demi Moore), convinces him that the accused Marine was most likely following an unwritten rule in hazing a fellow Marine which resulted in his death.

Fortunately, most unwritten rules in organizations are not as extreme; nonetheless at times we passively "go along, to get along."

Dependence: Over-dependence on our workplace for "a job for life" has weakened many of us. Even though dependent people lean on the hierarchy to sustain and support them, they don't like being powerless. They want the support yet bitterly resent the fact that they need it. People resent the presumption of incompetence that underlies dependence.

But without confidence, they remain dependent and more resentful than grateful. Thus, dependence has fed complacency.

This situation may partly explain why complacent people so often become greedy. In addition to grabbing for security, while boxed into resenting what they get, they unconsciously also seek to "get even" by demanding even more.

Creating Your Career / Denise O'Brien

As I was researching to write this book I had a most insightful conversation with a gentleman, whom I'll refer to as Mark on how feelings of dependency almost fed complacency in him. Mark informed me he knew it was time for him to leave his former workplace when he began to feel dependent upon it.

He had been working with the company for approximately 10 years and he was feeling a little restless, almost as though it might be time to seek other opportunities.

He recalls feeling hesitant to even consider leaving because his thoughts were focused on, "oh, but what will happen to my benefits?" In other words, Mark, like many others, had come to feel dependent upon the organization.

Some might argue that remaining with an organization to ensure ongoing health and retirement benefits is not about dependency. I absolutely agree that benefits considerations are critical to making informed decisions about "what's next?"

However, if you choose to stay, do not be bitter. Commit to following all of the advice I offered in Chapter 2 to learn to be your best self and to give your life purpose.

Greed: Complacent organizations create people who keep asking what else is going to be done for them…and it's never enough. These organizations also breed individuals who complain about what is being done "to" them.

Within these types of organizations there will tend to be a mentality of scarcity rather than abundance. In his book, *The 7 Habits of Highly Effective People,* [37] Dr. Stephen Covey explains the concepts of scarcity and abundance as follows:

---

[37] Stephen Covey, *The 7 Habits of Highly Effective People: Powerful Lessons in Personal Change*, (New York, Fireside, pp.219, 1990)

> *Most people are deeply scripted in what I call the Scarcity Mentality. They see life as having only so much, as though there were only one pie out there. And if someone were to get a big piece of the pie, it would mean less for everybody else. The Scarcity Mentality is the zero-sum paradigm of life. People with a Scarcity Mentality have a very difficult time sharing recognition and credit, power or profit—even with those who help in the production. They also have a hard time being genuinely happy for* the success of other people.[38]
>
> *The Abundance Mentality, on the other hand, flows out of a deep inner sense of personal worth or security. It is the paradigm that there is plenty out there and enough to spare for everybody. It results in the sharing of prestige, recognition, profits and decision-making. It opens possibilities, options, alternatives and creativity.*

Dr. Covey's point is that thinking we do not have enough—time, resources, staff, information, knowledge, whatever—influences us to compete for available resources, even when there is enough, or maybe even an abundance of them.

As I write this book, the world is confronting the deadly Coronavirus pandemic.

The scarcity mentality has reared its ugly head in some parts of the world as countries face growing concerns about the availability of lifesaving medical supplies.

---

[38] Drew Hendricks, "Four Steps to Stop Comparing Your Success to Others," *Success Magazine*

Even in parts of the world in which there is likely a sufficient amount of supplies, the public is hearing messages that "we don't have enough" and "there is no way we will share our supply." In other words, the scarcity mentality is not one of collaboration which leads to figuring out how we can make do with what we have; rather it generates an "us against them" approach to just about everything.

The Balancing Act of Complacency

Every day I come across at least one article or reference to mental health and the many ways in which our well-being is being impacted by too much stress and other factors.

Rarely do I come across articles that reference any of what I've covered in this chapter.

I believe complacency at work breeds fear and, as noted by Stephen Covey in the excerpt above, a "scarcity mentality," is detrimental to our personal well-being.

People are not energized to perform at their best when they are so cocooned in entitlement-thinking that they become complacent.

When people are dependent and receive without having to achieve they are protected from failure.

Growth is inhibited. When there are no consequences for mediocre performance we become entitled, passive, greedy… and complacent.

By insulating ourselves from risk and failing to hold ourselves to higher standards, we destroy our self-esteem.

If you are a parent reading this book, and you have ever had to push your child outside of his or her comfort zone, then you understand what I am talking about.

You understood this act of pushing your child outside their comfort zone was necessary action to take in order for him or her to grow, flourish, and learn to survive independent of you. And yet it likely felt painful.

The same holds true for making sure we don't become so stranded in our comfort zone at work that we feel dependent upon it.

Over the years, I have had many conversations with individuals who describe themselves as "stuck" in their organization, with no way out. I find this a fascinating description, given that free will is a societal value we generally embrace.

If you are feeling "stuck," I challenge you to reflect on the ties that are binding you to your organization. You may find you are "stuck" in complacency. Be mindful: this is not a pleasant place to stay for a long period of time.

How are you positioned for your future career?

You completed the Complacency Quiz earlier, which provided you with an idea of where you're positioned on the complacency continuum.

You now know it's not a good career decision to become complacent.

So, let's get you moving forward and leave complacency in the rearview mirror.

To help you assess how well you are positioned for your future career I invite you to complete the Career Positioning Quiz on the next page:

Creating Your Career / Denise O'Brien

Career Positioning Quiz		
Respond "yes" or "no" to the statements below.		
Statement	Yes	No
I have a good reputation, both inside my organization and outside in my profession.		
People call me for help and advice, and I try to help them.		
I know what I want or need to learn next and have spent my own money to enhance my career or expand my knowledge in the last year.		
I know the hot topics and trends in my field.		
I know what the next technical challenge will be in my field.		
I have a set of professional contacts I can call for help or support.		
I volunteer my time in a number of ways.		
I make it a point to keep my résumé up-to-date with my skills, experiences, and achievements		

Results:

If you can say "yes" to five or more of the statements above, you don't have to worry. You are well positioned to manage your career. If you didn't score well on this list, you can easily change things. Just begin doing what's described in the statements in this quiz. Start contributing to your colleagues, your community, your profession, and your professional network — and reputation — will expand accordingly.

Recap of Key Points

1. Even when people put in a lot of time, they do not always contribute much. They do not add a lot of value. They may be busy looking busy. They do not feel good about it. It robs them of dignity and feeds complacency and what I refer to as a "victim mentality."

2. Complacency is detrimental. It destroys motivation. It feeds fear. It stifles creativity and learning. It makes us feel entitled and greedy.

3. Complacency is not a new phenomenon. It is the legacy of years of affluence.

4. Organizations have unintentionally institutionalized complacency with ineffective performance management practices, reward and recognition programs, committees with no real purpose, compensation systems that do not seem fair, layers of bureaucracy and rules, and passivity.

5. People are not at their keenest when life is too safe and they are complacent. When people do not have to earn what they receive they are protected from failure. Growth is inhibited. When there are no consequences for mediocre performance we become mediocre, entitled, passive, greedy...and complacent.

6. By insulating ourselves from risk and failing to hold ourselves to higher standards of performance, we destroy our self-esteem.

Creating Your Career / Denise O'Brien

Best Advice and Tips to Navigate Complacency

Conducting interviews to research and write this book I heard much sage advice to help one navigate away from Complacency:

- It is harder to look busy than to actually be busy.

- There is nothing better than working hard – it feeds our soul, it gives us purpose and meaning, and it contributes to our well-being.

- Education only gets you so far – the rest comes from working hard.

- Keep moving – I mean this both literally and figuratively. In other words, challenge yourself every day to look for opportunities and ways you can contribute in your workplace. Complacency should not be a permanent state. Seize opportunities. Stay active – keep your brain and body moving.

- Busy-work does not equate to meaningful work. Know the difference.

- Set stretch goals for yourself and continue to push beyond your personal comfort zone. For example, if you have a fear of public speaking (which is very common for most of us), then find ways to become better a public speaker. Join a local speaking association, offer to facilitate or present at meetings, etc.

- The point is, when we push ourselves to learn new things, and develop skills, we move further away from complacency.

- Assume there is enough: approaching life and work with an attitude of "scarcity," and the idea there isn't enough, can lead us down a path of negativity and leave us feeling even further depleted. For example, many years ago I worked with a woman, whom I'll call "Maura. Maura was perpetually overwhelmed and went about her day with an attitude that "there isn't enough." She scrambled from one meeting to the next, lugging an armload of paperwork with her everywhere she went, and she often ate her lunch while scurrying around (because she didn't have time to take a proper lunch break she said.)

During meetings (for which she was mostly unprepared), she mostly riffled through her voluminous papers, focused on her voracious note-taking, or directed her attention to every distracting bing from her smartphone.

Maura tended to talk about "what's wrong" and say things like, "there's not enough." She'd scurry out of meeting rooms and rush off to her next meeting, complaining, "there isn't enough time in the day."

In truth, Maura's mantra that "there isn't enough" was actually the root of her problem. Had she simply changed her assumption and thus her mindset to "there is enough," then figured out her priorities, and gave them her undivided attention, Maura would have been less burdened at work.

Whenever you hear yourself saying things such as "there isn't enough time," "there isn't enough money," "there isn't enough information," etc., tune into that language, because it is a reflection of your thinking. I bet it isn't always serving you well.

- Live Within Your Means: I believe some of us become complacent, and settle in workplaces, not because we love the work itself, but rather because we feel – stuck. When we spend as much as we earn, and even more than we earn, we get buried in debt.

  Once we're in over our heads in debt we constrict our freedom to make different choices about our work. During my research, one very wise individual articulated it this way.

  > "Get out of debt – immediately! Stop buying stuff you don't need. It gives you choice."

- Get a Coach: If you are feeling stuck hire a career coach to help move forward.

- Get a Side Hustle: If you are not feeling satisfied with your current work, rather than becoming complacent explore entrepreneurial opportunities to fill some of your time outside of work. For example, during my research a teacher shared with me that since schools are closed during the summer, he spends those months operating a side-business of applying black top sealant to residential driveways. A firefighter mentioned he does home renovations when he's not working at his regular job.

Creating Your Career / Denise O'Brien

Chapter 5

Women

> ***Between what happens to us and our response is a space. In that space lies our freedom to choose our response.***
>
> **—Anonymous**

A number of years ago I was listening to the radio as I drove home from work. The station was playing a political debate in the federal house of commons. As I listened to the individuals argue back and forth I was struck by the realization that none of the voices belonged to women. Rather, the raised voices were male and all were spewing similar rhetoric. I recall thinking, "where are all the women?" It seemed unfathomable that women were apparently absent from these important conversations.

This experience fueled my curiosity about the status of women in our workplaces and this led me to conduct a field study. I interviewed women from varied backgrounds and job functions, including human resources, administration, public works, health care and first responders. I also conducted an extensive review of the literature available on this topic.

Although my study was conducted less than 10 years ago I am happy to write that even in this short amount of time I believe the landscape of work has changed significantly for women.

This chapter outlines some of the current research on women in the workplace and it also shares some of my own findings, based on the many conversations I've enjoyed with women about their careers.

Where are all the women?

According to a study entitled "Women in the Workplace 2019"[39] conducted jointly by McKinsey & Company and LeanIn.org, there has been progress in the representation of women in corporate America over the past five years. For example, the study says that since 2015 "the number of women in senior leadership has grown. This is particularly true in the C-suite, where the representation of women has increased from 17% to 21%."

Surely, this is good news?

Not so fast – the study points out that although this is progress and a step in the right direction, parity remains way off in the future, if ever. The results of the study found women, particularly women of colour, remain underrepresented at every level of management in workplaces.

In the following section I explore a bit of the research and offer explanations to explain why women remain underrepresented in management roles.

---

[39] "Women in the Workplace 2019," *McKinsey and Co*.

Research says ....

For many years it has been generally understood that a glass ceiling, or labyrinth, or some other artificial barrier based on attitudinal or organizational bias, continues to prevent qualified women from advancing upward in their organization. At this point I think it might be helpful to share a bit of an explanation about this terminology.

The term "glass ceiling" was first used in 1986 by two journalists – Carol Hymowitz and Timothy Schellhardt in the Wall Street Journal. It has come to be defined as a barrier that prevents qualified individuals from advancing within their organization and reaching their full potential.[40]

Some research argues the barrier is not a ceiling but rather a maze or labyrinth in which women find themselves trapped.[41]

Regardless of the metaphor one prefers, at the core of this issue is the possibility that bias may be getting in the way of women's career progress. Before I explore the possibility of bias, however, let me share some of the counter arguments put forward to explain the disproportionate number of men in management in our workplaces.

Educational Choices

Over the years I have heard the argument that the lack of representation is less about gender inequity and more a reflection of women's educational choices.

---

[40] R. Snyder, "The glass ceiling for women: Things that don't cause it and things that won't break it," *Human Resources Development Quarterly, Spring, 1993*, pp. 97-106, 1993

[41] Alice Eagly and Linda Carli, *Through the Labyrinth* (Boston, Harvard Business School Press, 2007)

In particular, women have traditionally opted to pursue studies in administrative or caregiving-type professions, which lead to lower-level organizational positions.

For example, Research conducted by Catalyst in 2016[42] found Canadian women represented only approximately one-third (34%) of all recipients of undergraduate degrees in science, technology, mathematics, and engineering (and according to the same research each of these paths are more likely to lead to more senior positions).

In other words, one explanation for the lack of women in senior positions is that traditionally many of us have tended to choose educational pursuits that do not necessarily lead to senior management roles.

Motivation and Life Choices

A fairly extensive body of literature has argued women have not moved up in organizations at the same rate as men because they make different life choices than men.

Susan Pinker writes in her book *The Sexual Paradox* (2008)[43] that women in general tend be motivated by intrinsic rewards such as feeling like they are making a difference, having the ability to contribute to their field, and enjoying the capacity to make a difference.

In other words, women tend to be motivated (and de-motivated) by how work makes them feel. Pinker notes the draw of intrinsic rewards and autonomy increases as women's level of education increase.[44]

---

[42] "Women in Science, Technology, Engineering, and Mathematics (STEM): Quick Take", *Catalyst*, June 14 2019

[43] Pinker, p, 70

[44] Susan Pinker, *The Sexual Paradox: Extreme Men, Gifted Women and the Real Gender G*ap (Vintage Canada, Toronto 2008)

As a result, women are more likely to "opt-out" of fulltime employment or choose to pursue careers at lower levels of pay and status because it feels more personally satisfying.

Males on the other hand have traditionally been more driven to satisfy extrinsic interests such as status and power. Furthermore, researcher R. A. Synder[45] notes in his research that men consistently value the status, prestige, and high incomes that are linked to their jobs. Thus motivation and interest lead males and females to make different work and life choices.

Gender – Traits and Characteristics

Feelings

According to Pinker (2008), women tend to be more sensitive to the emotional impact they have on others.

In addition, sociologists Catherine Ross and John Mirowsky[46] estimate women experience distress 30% more often than men.

Women also feel sadness, malaise and anxiety more acutely and more often than men. In other words, females are generally more emotional than males. Thus it seems reasonable that women are more predisposed to experience burnout and depression at rates higher than those experienced by men. Women, take note of this paragraph, and read on to manage your emotions.

---

[45] R.A. Synder, "The glass ceiling for women: Things that don't cause it and things that won't break it", Human Resources Quarterly, 4(1), 97-106, 1993

[46] J. Mirowsky and C.Ross, "Sex Differences in Distress: Real or Artifact?, "*American Sociological Review*, 60, 1995

In Chapter 3, I reviewed the importance of managing our emotions and looked at the ways in which poorly managed emotions at work can be a career-de-railer (not to mention how much they contribute to symptoms of burnout and depression).

Although both genders are susceptible to letting their emotions run amok in the workplace, personal experience has taught me women have to work even harder than men to be able to regulate their emotional responses.

Example:

> Martha is a highly seasoned professional with many years of experience. She currently works in a hospital on a team with 12 female staff members. Her manager, Rita, is seven years her junior. Martha and Rita get along fine, but Martha feels Rita does not take her job seriously and she is frequently absent from work attending to personal family matters. Martha often feels anger and frustration with Rita because of her approach to work.
>
> Rita is a single mother with two young children and she is currently going through a messy divorce. She finds Martha to be a dedicated professional, although it can be extremely difficult to work with her, as she often comes across as moody, sullen, and abrupt. Martha's negative demeanour has been noticed by her colleagues and they have told Rita they do not enjoy working with her. Rita knows she will have to speak to Martha about her attitude and the ways in which it is negatively impacting the team.
>
> In this scenario both women seem to have a lot on their respective plates. If you are a female employed in a workplace you can probably relate to the above scenario.

Managerial Traits

Historical and popular literature has tended to portray women as good communicators who are nurturing and supportive, while men have been described as more naturally aggressive, competitive, and independent.

A study by the Pew Research Center[47] revealed that some people believe the scarcity of women in top business positions is primarily due to the fact that women are innately not tough enough for business. Other research disputes this, and argues the problem is not that women are not tough enough, but rather that the gender biases at play within organizations detrimentally affect performance ratings — and therefore the general perceptions of whether women have what it takes to be promoted to upper-level positions.

It has been found that in general women (including women of colour) tend to be stigmatized as less capable than white males,[48] and they tend to have the ongoing burden of proving themselves competent and deserving.

Virginia Schein, a seasoned expert in the barriers women have experienced in career advancement, has reviewed and replicated research undertaken in the 1970s and found a "think manager-think male" phenomenon continues to permeate the selection and promotion of women globally.[49]

---

[47] Pew Research Center, "Men or women: Who's the better leader?" *Pew Research Center*

[48] "Women in the Workplace 2019," *McKinsey and Co.*

[49] Victoria Schein, "A Global Look at Psychological Barriers to Women's Progress in Management," *Journal of Social Issues*, 2001, pp. 675-688

The good news: there has been a gradual shift in belief systems around the acceptance of women; almost all of the women who have attained top positions in corporations around the world have done so from the 1990s and later, although there remains much room for progress.[50]

Double Bind

In truth women are in a "double bind:" on one hand they are expected to fulfill the stereotypical female gender role by being warm and selfless, and on the other hand, they are also expected to fulfill a leadership role by displaying assertiveness and competence. It is a dilemma that can lead women to feel conflicted.

Alice Eagly and Linda Carli[51] are researchers and educators who have investigated this phenomenon and have found that assertive women are usually described in derogatory ways such as "bitch" while assertive men are labeled "passionate," or "driven."

Whichever way a female leader acts, she is perceived as going against either the norms of good leadership or the norms of femininity. As a result, women are often in a no-win situation, which can seriously influence their career choices. These choices have both short-term and much longer-term implications.

It can certainly be argued that stereotypes and subtle, often hidden forms of discrimination continue to limit women's advancement, even though many organizations refuse to acknowledge discriminatory practices that might exist within their walls. With the retirement of members of the baby-boom

---

[50] Sheryl Sandberg, *Lean In: Women, Work and the Will to Lead* (New York, Alfred A. Knopf, 2013)

[51] Alice Eagly and Linda Carli, *Through the Labyrinth* (Boston, Harvard Business School Press, 2007)

generation — and the skills shortages that will result—organizations must develop solid recruitment and retention strategies at leadership levels that do in fact include women.

Since women comprise approximately 50% of the labour force — and in many fields they have a higher rate of university graduation than men — it seems they should be an obvious leadership resource that at present is not fully tapped. Giving greater attention to women and the talents they bring to the workplace serves both the individual and the organization well.

The sheer volume of the research on this topic that has been undertaken over the years suggests a genuine societal interest in understanding why men are more likely to succeed to senior management positions than are women.

Much of the research and the literature is so compelling and reasonable that one might simply agree, for example, that the reason fewer women hold senior management positions than men is because they have different priorities and values, and this leads them to make different choices.

It can also be argued from an evolutionary perspective that women are more naturally drawn to being home taking care of babies or being caretakers of the elderly and the infirm. While this may seem reasonable, it leaves one to wonder why these same women continue to flood university classrooms to complete post-secondary and graduate level studies. Are they temporarily fighting their biological instincts? In other words, the research, while plentiful, may in some respects be too simplistic, and it is actually dismissive of potentially damaging inequities in the treatment of human beings based solely on gender.

Research gathered over the last decade in particular illustrates that while the personal choices of some women may explain the rate at which they succeed to the most senior levels in organizations, stereotyping and subtle, often *hidden,* forms of discrimination are significant factors limiting women's advancement.

Keep in mind that the act of stereotyping is not necessarily done with intent, malice, or some form of blatant prejudice. Rather, gender stereotypes are common, and they are often applied as a result of accepted cultural, societal, or unconscious beliefs about women or women's role in the workplace.

While the foregoing looks at more or less "official academic" explanations of why men have tended to ascend to higher levels of power within organizations, conversations with women turn up other key aspects of the issue. Here's what women have told me directly:

Succession Planning

In my many conversations with women about their careers—and in particular their individual experiences and feelings associated with the glass ceiling — a general mood of dissatisfaction and frustration has tended to emerge.

Many refer to "succession planning" activities — or the lack thereof — within their organization as an important part of the equation.

More specifically, they feel it is the lack of formal planning, goal setting, and performance development in their organization that prevents them from moving forward in their careers.

In the absence of transparent succession planning procedures, women generally perceive men are being considered to be more viable candidates than they are, which means their own careers are being stalled at lower levels in the organization.

Career Aspirations

Another consideration for many women is the lack of clearly articulated personal career plans and goals.

When asked about their career aspirations and professional goals, women generally express that they do not have specific goals or aspirations. Even women who feel they have broken through the glass ceiling indicate they generally do not have a clear perception of what they want to achieve in their professional lives. In other words, they tend to have a serendipitous approach to personal career planning.

Even though most women I have spoken with about careers indicate they have no actual goal, we (myself included) often continue taking courses and participate in non-work activities to "build our résumés" and "prove our worth." If no link exists between course studies, extracurricular activities and your career aspirations, then you may be wasting precious time and money.

This approach to career may well be contributing to significant career derailment and other challenges. For example, some women have expressed frustration over the fact they have put forth effort to take courses, but this has not advanced their career.

Stop! Stop taking courses unless they are required for a position you aspire to attain. Stop feeling as though you have to prove yourself. You are amazing just the way you are!

In conducting my research I enjoyed conversations with amazing women who have enjoyed successful careers despite having embarked upon the journey without much forethought or planning about where they wanted to go or who they wanted to become in the process.

The good news is that as a result of not having a clear goal in mind, women tend to respond quite spontaneously to opportunities as they occur. Seizing opportunities is a wonderful thing. Be mindful, however, that "no plan" is not the ideal situation and tends to lead towards dissatisfaction with career and life.

I encourage you to balance a "seize the day" approach with a high degree of self-awareness and planning: if you have no idea where you're going, how will you know when you have arrived?

Role Modeling

Another common theme I discovered during my many conversations with women was the lack of female role models in the senior ranks of organizations. Many have told me this is a barrier because it gives the impression women are not welcome. It also tends to make females feel less confident about their capabilities. It makes them more hesitant, as it feels scary to be breaking new ground.

In addition to women not feeling sure about what was expected with respect to behaviours that were appropriate for women as compared to men, I found there was sometimes a theme at play of women being less tolerant of other women, as well. For example, one woman mentioned she worked better with men because her experience had led her to believe that women tend to have more insecurities than men, which they felt tended to create strained working relationships.

Again, as noted above these feelings and experiences are not unlike the "double-bind" perspective introduced earlier. Essentially, women in leadership roles are put in the position of being judged and criticized if they are too friendly or too consultative rather than coming across as a "take charge" person able to convey assertion and control.

In other words, no matter how they perform and behave, women are more likely to leave the impression they do not have the right skillset to lead. Women in the workplace judge other women as harshly as men do, and often even more so.[52]

Consequences and Impacts

During my conversations with women to explore the existence of the glass ceiling – real or imagined — I heard repeatedly that women do not ascend to the highest levels in their organizations at the same rate as males because men and women make different choices which may lead to unintended outcomes and consequences. Here's more about that:

1. **An Uneven Playing Field for Women**
   Some women noted that an uneven playing field limits their career options and the opportunities available to them, particularly with respect to promotions and upward mobility.

   Here are some of the issues that relate to a perceptively uneven playing field:

   - **Gender De-selection**
     Some women believe that as a result of systemic bias they are viewed as less valuable or capable simply because they are female and therefore they feel they are considered to be less viable candidates for promotions, particularly to senior leadership positions. (Recall the notion of "think-manager-think male" mentioned earlier in this chapter.)

---

[52] Candy Deemer and Nancy Fredericks, *Dancing on the Glass Ceiling: Tap Into Your True Strengths, Activate Your Vision, and Get What You Really Want out of Your Career* (New York, McGraw Hill, 2002)

- **Work is Not Valued Equally**

  It has been pointed out to me that some work, professions or career fields where women have traditionally been more numerous—such as human services and homemakers— are simply less valued. For example, roles such as nursing, caregiving, human resources, and homemaking are traditionally performed predominantly by women and there have been disparities in the value some have placed on these roles. There is definitely research to support the accuracy of this perception.[53] Fortunately, I see shifts on this front.

- **Networking inequities**

  The ease with which a woman can access networking opportunities also has an impact upon her career. For instance, many women have pointed out that as a result of their demanding work and home lives they miss out on opportunities to network and feel this has had a significant negative outcome on their career advancement opportunities.

  Despite many positive societal changes, women continue to assume much of the responsibility for the home, although many have spouses who contribute more than men of earlier generations did. For example, one woman mentioned her husband did much of the housework, shopping and cooking, yet she still felt that the majority of responsibilities for their home and personal life resided with her.

---

[53] "Women in the Workplace 2017," *McKinsey and Company*

The reality is, if you want access to the most senior positions in your organization, networking and nurturing your contacts are critical. In their extensive research Alice Eagly and Linda Carli found that socializing with colleagues and building professional networks—often considered "nonessential" aspects of work—create a social capital that turns out to be quite essential indeed.

They use an example to illustrate the point. Or, as a prominent female executive told one of us, "You don't want to be 'Jane the Drudge,' sitting in your office and just working all the time. You have to gain visibility and recognition for your work" by getting out there."[54]

2. Work Style Differences

- **Caring Versus Caring Too Much**
  During my research, women repeatedly shared stories about the deep "care" they feel about their work. This is a "good news/bad news" issue.

  As noted earlier in this chapter, women tend to be drawn to, and motivated by, work that makes them feel as though they are contributing and making a difference. These feelings of making a difference help give us

---

[54] Eagly and Carli, p. 150

purpose, which feeds our soul. This is about doing and giving and caring. Perhaps this way of working might be described as exerting "labours of love" which is, of course, a "good news story."

On the flip side, though, is "the bad news" about caring too much. Over the years many of the women I have spoken with often feel as though they are working harder than others, and are creating more tangible results than those achieved by their male colleagues.

Many have expressed to me the fact that they feel they are better than their male counterparts at fostering collaborative, positive relationships, which they regard as very important to being a positive role model and making a difference. In other words, many of us women feel genuinely concerned about work outputs and thus we fully apply ourselves to make sure things get done.

In the meantime, we can be walking on eggshells to avoid hurting anyone's feelings while ensuring we are good team players. As a result, we might actually begin to harbour some ill-will towards our colleagues which, of course, we do not express. We can feel quite put out when others do not even seem to notice or appreciate our efforts and our martyrdom.

Let me provide an example to help illustrate this point. In my household I feel as though I do most of the "household chores" including shopping, cleaning, meal preparation, making sure medical appointments are taken care of, and chauffeuring family members to sporting activities. From time-to-time, I may perceive my spouse as doing less than his fair share. This especially occurs when I am tired and feeling a little overwhelmed. At these times, I might not say anything but rather carry on, feeling quite annoyed I am doing more than my fair share. Do you get my point?

I see myself as caring more than my husband does and rather than have a conversation with him about my perceptions of the distribution of the household chores, I persevere even though it is not in my best interest to do so. This same phenomenon happens in our workplaces as well.

And, as I listened to women describe their experiences with the glass ceiling, there was a consistent strong undercurrent of resentment and frustration bubbling just beneath the surface (in much the same way I feel resentment toward my husband when I choose not to distribute the household chores more equitably).

Some women have acknowledged they often consciously work at not being resentful and try to keep resentment from seeping into their professional lives. It is discouraging for them to feel like they "care so much" in organizations they perceive as "uncaring." Tune in to these feelings, as they are giving you very important messages about the choices you might be making.

- **Proving Worth**
  Women repeatedly referenced the idea of "proving myself," which they felt motivated them to work harder than their male counterparts. For example, one woman indicated she often felt like she was "riding a roller coaster." She would work hard to prove herself and then become frustrated and subsequently put forth only minimal effort. Again, feeling like we have to work harder to "prove ourselves" leads to feelings of resentment, frustration, and anger. The irony is that females choose to work hard, yet feel resentment for making this choice. Stop! Stop feeling as though you have to prove yourself! You are enough.

3. **The Old Boys' Club**
   Another barrier that has gotten in the way of women's career advancement relates to systemic issues, such as "the Old Boys' Club." This term refers to a variety of activities that exclude women, such as lunches to which only men are invited, and meetings that occur on the golf course, in the men's room, or over beer and chicken wings. Some women view these behaviours as unintentional while others regard them as blatant and overt.

   During my research, women characterized members of the Old Boys' Club as being male, often Caucasian, middle-aged, educated, and endowed with enough savvy to engage in "political game-playing." Some noted that since men typically hold the positions of power in an organization, they tend to select males who look and sound like themselves. These male newcomers are more easily admitted, encultured, and accepted into the Club.

Creating Your Career / Denise O'Brien

Example:

Darla is 42 years old and has worked in her current organization for seven years. She is bright, hardworking, and keen to move up in the organization.

The company she works for is expanding and she has taken on additional responsibilities and work, without much additional compensation.

Ultimately, Darla aspires to be the company's Chief Financial Officer (CFO) and she has worked really hard to prove she has the capabilities.

For example, Darla even filled the CFO role for three months last year when the current CFO was off on a short-term medical leave.

During that time, Darla received only positive feedback from the President. When the CFO announced his retirement three months ago Darla was excited and optimistic. She regarded herself as the perfect candidate, particularly since she had proven herself already by doing the job on an interim basis.

When the CFO vacancy was posted, Darla naturally applied for the position. Ultimately, the President did not select Darla. He chose a male friend with whom he had attended university and with whom he now continued to interact socially. These men were similar in age, education, and cultural background and were a mirror image of each other. Darla was devastated.

In this scenario, Darla made the assumption that she was passed over for the more senior role because of the "Old Boys' Club." It is hard to know for sure what motivated the president of the company to refrain from selecting Darla. Maybe the other candidate had better skills, knowledge and experiences. Either way, Darla was at a crossroad in her work journey and she had to make the choice to:

- Accept the president's decision, set aside her disappointment, stay with the company, and build a harmonious, respectful relationship with the incoming CFO or,
- Look for a position with another company.

To choose anything else, such as staying with the company feeling bitter and resentful, would likely cause Darla's career to de-rail. (Staying when it might be time to leave is discussed in more detail in Chapters 6 and 7.)

4. Different Expectations and Standards for Women

In addition to "the Old Boys' Club," I have heard from many women that they feel confusion about what is expected of them by others; they also feel uncertain about what they expect for, and of, themselves. In fact, women often feel as though there are different expectations and standards for women than there are for men.

For example, one woman felt she would not get away with the same behaviours as her male counterparts, particularly with regard to what these men tended to say, and to whom. She felt her boss was much more tolerant of assertive behaviours from her male colleagues than would be tolerated and deemed acceptable if she behaved the same way. Recall the concept of the "double-bind," a dilemma women have commonly experienced in their work-life journeys.

However, on this front I believe women have made, and continue to make significant progress. I attribute progress to a number of factors, including amendments to workplace Health and Safety legislation and Human Rights laws.

These have given women a greater voice and more protection against such things as being terminated without cause and being able to take leaves of absences for maternity and sickness without having to worry about their job. In addition, societal movements such as #MeToo have succeeded in further levelling the playing field for women.

Fuelled largely through social media platforms, the #MeToo movement has inspired women (and men) to say "no" to harassment, discrimination, inequities and other forms of mistreatment.

It is inspiring to see how quickly the messages coming out of the #MeToo movement have taken hold in North American society. It is hard to realize that the phrase was only spoken for the first time in 2006 by a social activist and community organizer named Tarana Burke. Her goal was to promote "empowerment through empathy" among women who had experienced sexual abuse, particularly those who were people of colour and belonged to underprivileged communities.

Later, in October 2017, actress Alyssa Milano popularized the term after she encouraged women to tweet #MeToo on social media to "give people a sense of the magnitude of the problem."

With a few high-profile cases in the media, the term #MeToo has influenced radical changes in the landscape of work, particularly for women.

Final Thoughts

I have devoted a chapter in this book to women because I believe women face distinct challenges along the work-life journey.

As mentioned earlier, women face a "double bind" as they navigate their work and personal lives. If women make work their priority, it often takes a toll on their personal lives.

Conversely, if women make their personal lives—including spouses, partners, children, family and non-work-related activities—their priority there are often negative consequences.

Another reality is that regardless of which choices they make, women tend to feel a sense of guilt.

For example, if a woman chooses to put matters related to her children and personal life ahead of work-related issues, and she misses work to take care of an ill child, she may second guess her choice and even feel guilty about it.

Women really do face many conundrums as they try to make the best choices for themselves, for their loved ones, and for their workplaces.

I often hear and read about struggles women experience with work-life balance. As a female, I too have traipsed along the same tightrope. Let me share how I got a handle on the work-life balance issue.

Example:

As I was driving to work one day, I felt a pain in my shoulder when I turned my head to check for oncoming traffic.

Maneuvering my neck and shoulders to check the traffic while turning the steering wheel felt painful.

I could not figure out what had triggered the pain because I had not engaged in any strenuous physical activities.

Upon reflection I realized that throughout my adult life the pain in my shoulder had appeared at times when I've been feeling overwhelmed and stressed.

I recall thinking, "I don't think I am stressed. What do I have to be stressed about?"

It prompted me to consider the length of my "to do list." I worked fulltime, volunteered approximately 30 hours per week with three agencies, I was completing my studies towards my graduate degree, and I was doing my best to be available for my family.

Needless to say, I realized my "to do list" was too long and it was taking a toll on my personal well-being. In that moment, I figured out that the list needed to be pared down to be more realistic.

I asked myself – how do I want to be spending my time? What are my priorities?

I came to the conclusion that family, work and completing the graduate studies were the order of my priorities and thus I needed to end my volunteer work.

I subsequently withdrew from my volunteer activities because it was not the right time for me to be taking on extra work when I already had enough on my plate.

The choices I was making about what I was saying "yes" to were not wise. I had taken on more than I realistically or physically was able to complete.

I was working hard, and putting in lots of time to get things done, but I was not being wise, and I certainly was not being kind to myself.

If I was spending time at volunteer activities, I was not available for my family, and coursework deadlines might get missed.

It was a vicious cycle of saying "yes" to things which were not urgent, important or even a priority for me – at times when I should have been saying "no, thank you."

The key to maintaining a healthy balance in work and life is to be honest about your priorities and learn to say "no thank you" to tasks, activities, opportunities, or invitations that are incongruent with your priorities.

Oh yes, the other important aspect of this is to learn to say, "no, thank you" and feel good about it. This seems more of an issue for women than for men, and it's high time we stopped feeling guilty and second guessing our choices.

Don't worry. You'll figure it out.

Recap of Key Points

1. It has been argued that women have traditionally tended to choose educational pursuits that do not always lead to senior management.

2. Women in general tend be motivated by intrinsic rewards such as feeling like they are contributing to their field or making even a small difference, or having an impact in the world. In other words, women tend to be motivated (and de-motivated) by "how work makes them feel."

3. Both genders are susceptible to letting their emotions run amok in the workplace. My personal experience leads me to believe women have to work even harder than men to regulate their emotional responses.

4. It has been found that women tend to be considered less capable than white males and they tend to have the ongoing burden of proving themselves to be competent and deserving. A "think-manager-think-male" phenomenon continues to permeate the selection and promotion of women globally. However, this mentality is gradually shifting and I estimate more and more women will ascend to the highest levels in organizations in the years to come.

5. Women tend to take a serendipitous approach to personal career planning which lends itself to feelings of frustration and uncertainty.

6. The "Old Boys' Club" still exists. Nonetheless, women are making great strides. Progress has been aided by changes in human rights and workplace health safety laws. The #MeToo movement has made great inroads towards helping level the playing field for women.

Best Advice and Tips for Women

- Stop taking courses unless they are linked to a specific career path. (Unless you are taking them for pure fun and enjoyment – in which case, carry on!)

- If you want access to the most senior positions in your organization, contacts and networking are critical.

- Be mindful to care about your work (whatever form your work takes) but be careful about caring too much: it can lead to some negative consequences.

- Stop feeling as though you have to prove yourself. You are enough!

- Stop being so hard on yourself. You are resilient, persistent, determined, caring, flexible and capable. You've got this!

- Finally, one of the absolute best pieces of advice I ever received came from a wise, elderly woman who began her career in the early 1960's and retired more than 45 years later. Her advice to women is this "No matter how you feel – Get up, Dress up and Never give up." Love it!

Chapter 6

Plateauing in Our Careers

> *Feeling plateaued should be a phase not a permanent state.*
>
> —**Judith Bardwick, PhD**

Have you ever heard the term "career plateau"? I have included a chapter on this topic because I believe it is one the most important — and perhaps most misunderstood — phases of one's career.

Career Plateau – Say What?

The term "career plateau" originated in the 1970s in the research of Thomas Ference, James Stoner, and Kirby Warren.[55] Plateauing occurs in different forms in all phases of our lives.

>Being plateaued is not a state of failure.

>Rather, it indicates we have arrived at a point in our work where we feel as though further progression is not possible, or no longer satisfying or of interest.

---

[55] T. Ference, J. Stoner and K. Warren, "Managing the Career Plateau," *Academy of Management Review*, 1977, pp. 602-612

The essential source of dissatisfaction and angst lies in the fact that the present feels unfulfilling and the future is not clear. When we've arrived at a career plateau we feel as though we are neither rising nor falling.

We may feel "stuck" or at least permanently stalled. We might ask ourselves,

"Is this all there is?"

"How much longer can I do this?"

"How many more years before I can retire?"

Types of Career Plateau

There are at least two types of career plateau: Organizational and Function-Related.

Organizational Plateaus

If you have arrived at an organizational plateau, you have come to the realization that you are unable to rise further in the organization's hierarchal structure. You have reached a point where the likelihood of additional upward movement—i.e. promotion—is very low.

An organizationally-plateaued employee who equates career success with hierarchical movement is likely to become upset even acknowledging that he or she has arrived at a plateau with their current employer. Such an employee may take action to remove themselves from the situation.

For instance, he or she might withdraw from organizational involvement, and lower his or her productivity. All of these scenarios provide a rationale for explaining why career plateauing often has a negative connotation.

I consider arriving at an organizational plateau to be an important moment in a career: who you have become through learning, effort, and experiences has helped you evolve to the point where you have outgrown the organization. When this occurs, it can feel like you are being held back, or constrained, by the organizational structure itself.

Think of it as being similar to getting bigger but still trying to squeeze into clothes that are a few sizes too small. It does not feel comfortable. However, keep in mind that arriving at an organizational plateau is a natural consequence of time, change, and personal growth, or a combination of all of these factors.

Example:

> After graduating from medical school at a young age Derek became a highly successful orthopedic surgeon working in a well-respected medical facility.
>
> Over the years, Derek had found his work extremely gratifying, particularly because he had opportunities to conduct ongoing research which were balanced with regular interaction with patients.
>
> He took great pride in being able to make a positive difference in the lives of his patients.
>
> Over the past two years or so, Derek has brought forward ideas to grow the practice, but they have been met with resistance from his Senior Director.

At this point, Derek is feeling as though he is "spinning his wheels" because the organization is not open to considering his ideas or looking for innovations in medical practices.

Although Derek is keen to advance his career, and he has aspirations to ascend to the top leadership of the medical facility in which he works, the current leadership seems to be overlooking his potential. Derek has grown so frustrated that last week he "blew up" at his boss.

Derek appears to have outgrown his organization. For years he had found satisfaction in his work but as time went on, he had aspirations to grow in his profession in ways that did not align with how his boss saw the organization evolving and growing.

Derek's frustrations grew to the extent that he acted inappropriately with his boss—not a wise career move. Can you relate to Derek's story?

Function-Related Plateau

Another possible work-related plateau is a job function plateau. Dr. Judith Bardwick in her book, The Plateauing Trap[56] points out that employees plateau in terms of function when either the likelihood they will continue to grow, or the opportunities for challenge associated with their current job, are low.

Function-plateaued employees may already be proficient in their jobs, and they expect no further challenges to be associated with the job; they tend to feel stifled with regards to the job's role, responsibilities, duties, etc.

---

[56] J. M. Bardwick, *The Plateauing Trap* AMACOM, New York, 1986)

Function-plateaued employees are no longer intrigued by their work and often feel they have reached a dead end. That is not to say there is nothing left for the individual to learn in the role. The opposite may be true. However, the individual may have lost interest in the job function itself, and putting forth effort to stay abreast of changes to the profession is unappealing.

Example:

> Kelly is a 50-year old woman and a "team leader" for an administrative team comprised of five women.
>
> Although she is responsible for delegating tasks, and she is the first point of contact for the other administrative staff members, Kelly is not considered "management." Her scope of authority and level of responsibility are limited. She is well-educated, bright, hard-working, and always willing to help when asked.
>
> Because she catches on quickly to new technologies and she is always willing to help others, Kelly has become the "go-to" person in the office. In the past, she made it known she was available to answer questions any time of the day or night, including weekends and holidays.
>
> Lately, Kelly has begun to express anger and frustration towards her manager and co-workers. She resents being asked to do tasks management staff should be doing.
>
> For the most part, while at work Kelly now feels a hair trigger away from reacting at any given moment.

Why has Kelly started expressing frustration and anger at work? What has caused her behaviour to change from reflecting an "above and beyond" approach to helping her colleagues to one that comes across as passive-aggressive? It may be that Kelly has plateaued in her work environment.

She mastered her job and, with energy to spare, she took on management activities without any opportunity for formal recognition from the organization in the form of advancement, increased compensation, status, or title.

Kelly has reached a job function plateau and is feeling constrained, and perhaps not fully appreciated by the organization for which she works.

Hitting A Plateau Can Kickstart a Vicious Cycle

Career plateauing is an important issue to get our heads around because of the potentially negative outcomes that will inevitably affect both the employee and the organization.

Career plateauing is likely to cause negative attitudes about work and feelings of disappointment and frustration.

In particular, plateaued employees are often described as displaying low levels of job involvement and work motivation.

Interestingly, plateaued employees may become less involved in their job because they believe the organization has devalued their contributions and they don't feel as though the organization cares about them or fully appreciates them.

As the employee feels increasingly dissatisfied with the organization and his or her work, they naturally feel less engaged in their work.

Reduced engagement correlates with lower job productivity, and so plateauing has been found to be negatively related to performance. In other words, a vicious cycle of assumptions, negativity and time wasting ensues.

Specific Impacts of Arriving at a Plateau:

Reduced Job Involvement: In my experience, employees who have hit a plateau report lower job involvement than their non-plateaued counterparts. This is not surprising, given that the individual feels disinterested, unfulfilled, unchallenged, inadequately rewarded, and unable to see opportunities for advancement.

Reduced Work Satisfaction: Understandably, plateaued employees will typically report low levels of job satisfaction and career satisfaction. Employees who are either organizationally plateaued or functionally plateaued tend to have lower levels of personal development-related satisfaction. It is not surprising, then, that hitting both organizational and function-related plateaus are negatively related to both job and career satisfaction. Individuals at this point will tend to feel "stuck."

Increased Turnover Rate: Plateaued employees are restless and thus may have a greater likelihood of leaving the organization. Plateauing has a negative effect on individual commitment to the organization and results in a loss of employee morale and productivity, which leads to turnover. And this can prove very costly to an organization.

Creating Your Career / Denise O'Brien

Note to Employers:

Once an employee has arrived at a work-related plateau it is important to recognize the resulting changes in his or her behaviour and performance for what they are: symptoms of a plateaued individual. I encourage you to support the individual to pursue opportunities, even those outside of your organization and will result in the loss of the employee to another company.

There are benefits to be reaped from this approach. Firstly, you build up goodwill with the individual who may leave your company and return at a future point with additional skills and expertise. This is referred to as a "boomerang" effect in talent management. The other obvious benefit is that if you hold the individual back from his or her career pursuits you are likely to be holding on to a complacent employee – definitely not a huge asset to the company, and it might even be a liability.

Personal impact: While an organization may experience negative repercussions when an employee experiences a plateau, the employee may also realize some personal consequences. Harmful psychological effects include lower self-worth due to the fact that promotions have been taken away, lower skill assessment, and less acceptance by peers and superiors due to devalued work contributions. Plateaued employees may be negatively stereotyped as "deadwood," and therefore neglected by supervisors and avoided by coworkers.

Think back to my discussion of Complacency in Chapter 4. I believe if we stay too long at a plateau in our work, we can move into complacency. Be mindful of staying too long at a plateau!

Arriving at a Career Plateau

It is conceivable that the reasons for organizational and function-related plateauing should be considered work stressors. This may be particularly true when the reason for becoming plateaued is outside the employee's control. For example, organizationally plateaued employees may become distressed upon acknowledging there are no more available positions; that is, there are organizational constraints disallowing further promotions.

It is quite conceivable the mismatch between the number of available positions — due to shorter corporate ladders — and the number of professional employees desiring to advance within an organization represents a significant source of stress.

Employees may become distressed should they perceive that the organization has negatively assessed their abilities and therefore has structurally plateaued them for organizational assessment reasons.

Function-plateaued employees may respond similarly when they acknowledge their jobs will no longer be challenging or that they offer little growth, little flexibility, or few increases in job responsibility. Dr. Bardwick makes the point that the end of job challenge can generate as much stress as the end of the hierarchical or structural climb. In Chapter 7 and 8 I discuss the exit phase of work and the psychological implications associated with this phase of our work-life journey.

Many of us in North America grew up defining success in terms of attaining more: more education, more power, more money, more responsibility, more status. This phenomenon is particularly true of the Silent Generation, the Baby Boomers, and Generation Xers. We learned that the way to achieve more was to move up the corporate ladder.

As a society we have come to believe that more = success. In other words, to be successful one must attain the highest level possible within the organization. Wow! That's a lot of pressure. It is also not very realistic, or even possible.

For now, and for some time into the future, far fewer people will experience the "success" of promotion. The post-depression period of economic growth and prosperity has dissipated. Companies which were in a growth phase following the Great Depression are either non-existent today or have radically streamlined operations, and they have removed layers of management.

Think back to Dr. Kai-Fu Lee's predictions around how AI will affect work and job loss. As we noted in Chapter 2, he points out many sectors — such as manufacturing — where human talent has been, and will continue to be, replaced by technological innovations such as AI, and robots.

When we are plateaued, our growth ambition, which, for many of us represents the main thrust of our career, is no longer an asset because it cannot be achieved in our current environment. That is when frustration spills out over everything that is most important, including our sense of self-esteem, our relationships, our performance, and our future prospects. In short, everything we have tended to define as "success" is perceived as lost or unattainable.

In my experience, unfortunately, most individuals and organizations do not recognize or understand that career plateauing is a natural phase we all reach at some point during our working life. In fact, plateauing is one phase of the process of change that is characteristic of everyone's life. No exceptions!

The only difference among people relates to how long they take to reach the level beyond which they will not rise. Keep in mind that in one form or another, everyone plateaus and, over the course of a lifetime, most of us will arrive at different plateaus, at different points in our lives.

Feelings of Stress at a Career Plateau

Think back to the examples of Derek and Kelly described earlier in the chapter. Derek had arrived at an organizational plateau and Kelly was at a job function plateau; both likely experienced similar feelings, including frustration and stress. Researchers[57] have found that stress regarding career progression may be equal among people of various careers and are more prevalent among professionals in the early stage of their career.

Both male and female employees have come to expect the same chances for career progression (thank you #MeToo for levelling the playing field for women). Since the organization is essentially removing those opportunities, or at least putting up perceived roadblocks, individuals understandably become distressed when they realize they have plateaued.

---

[57] S. Heilmann, D. Holt and C. Rilovick, "Effects of Career Plateauing on Turnover: A Test Model," *Journal of Leadership & Organizational Studies*, 2008, pp. 59-68

Self-Diagnosis – Feeling Plateaued at Work

In the examples of Derek and Kelly we referenced earlier, it's well to keep in mind that their change in behaviour will likely go "undiagnosed" by the organization.

An employee's change in performance at work is often perceived by management as being the result of a bad attitude, an unwillingness to change, a preference for being difficult, some personal problems and my absolute favourite: mental health issues. The truth is, very few of us recognize when we have arrived at a career plateau.

Furthermore, most of us are psychologically unprepared for the almost inevitable pain associated with arriving at the point in our work where we do not see any more challenges ahead or we've ascended as high we can go in the organization or career. Because we don't understand what is happening, anxiety, frustration, anger and feelings of hopelessness are at the forefront as we go through our workday.

My guess is that Derek and Kelly are unaware of what lies at the heart of their feelings of frustration. The trick is to know when you have plateaued because that awareness can turn the state of being plateaued into the springboard to launch you into the next phase of a wonderful life.

Exercise: I invite you to do the Plateau Questionnaire below to self-diagnose whether you may be at a plateau in your work. How many of the statements relate to how you're feeling?

Creating Your Career / Denise O'Brien

PLATEAU QUESTIONNAIRE: Beside each statement put a check mark in the column relating how you are feeling – either "Sounds like me" or "Does not sound like me." There are no right or wrong answers. So be honest.		
	✓ **Sounds like me**	✓ **Doesn't sound like me**
1. I'm going through the motions at work		
2. I keep the seat warm, only		
3. My work matters		
4. I'm stuck		
5. I look forward to going to work		
6. I feel good about my work		
7. I push paper around		
8. I make a valuable contribution		
9. Nothing ever changes		
10. I feel energized about my work		
11. I find work draining		
12. Nobody else cares. Why should I?		
13. I think about work as, "every day is a pensionable day"		
14. I have no new challenges		
15. Same old, same old		
16. I love my work		
17. I see lots of opportunities for advancement at work		
18. I see lots of opportunities for learning and growth		

Results:
You are likely not at a plateau in your work if you selected;
> "Sounds like me" – 3, 5, 6, 8, 10, 16, 17, 18 and
> "Does not sound like me" – 1,2, 4, 7,9,11,12,13,14 , 15

Compare the statements you selected, against the "ideal" results. Are you at a plateau? Is it an organizational plateau or a function-related plateau?

Note: Another good way to self-diagnose whether you might be at a career plateau is to look back to Chapter 4 and review how well you did on the complacency quiz. Sometimes, when we have arrived at a plateau we can feel stuck — either because we have outgrown the organization or the work itself. This can contribute to complacency. In other words, complacency can be a by-product of arriving at a plateau in our work.

Over the years, career plateauing has been the subject of studies to measure and potentially predict the point and time in one's career at which a person is likely to arrive at a career plateau. In truth, I don't think there is any reliable way to know for sure when a person will plateau in his or her career.

In my experience, one's age and the length of time one has spent doing the work influences the point at which a career plateau is reached. Keep in mind that objective measures such as age and length of time in the role should be taken as "food for thought," rather than hard-and-fast confirmations of the exact timing of our arrival at a career plateau.

For example, during my research, I spoke with a gentleman, whom I'll refer to Alex. Alex had been the Supervisor of the same work unit for 19 of the 23 years of his career.

I was curious to understand whether Alex was still as passionate about his work as he had been when he started 19 years earlier because his situation struck me as unusual. In my experience, most people will arrive at a career plateau long before 19 years have passed.

However, Alex seemed very content and was still quite engaged in his work. Thus, career plateaus are unique to individuals and their circumstances.

Predicting how long it might take for one to arrive at a career plateau is difficult for at least three reasons:

Reason #1

Chronological age and length of tenure will vary from industry to industry, and these measures fail to capture the notion of a stalled career. When is one stalled? How can age or tenure be a proxy when individuals often move from company to company, or through myriad industries, and then restart their careers at a senior age?

Reason #2

Objective measures fail to capture one's personal perception of being plateaued. Plateauing seems to run along a continuum where some individuals perceive being plateaued sooner than others.. However, since most organizations have streamlined, rightsized, outsourced, downsized, or reorganized over the past 20 years, I foresee that going forward, employees will plateau much earlier in their careers than they did in previous years.

Reason #3

Hand-in-hand with organizational restructuring has been the elimination of many jobs, and there has been a particular emphasis on the streamlining and culling of management functions.

As management roles have been eliminated, so too have opportunities for advancement, which means the management pipeline has become bottle-necked with potential candidates to fill the management functions but there are few roles to be filled. In other words, it is not unusual for organizations to develop employees to be ready to move into management positions "as they become available."

However, the rate at which people develop is not always relative to the potential internal demand and, as a result, there are more potential candidates than there are positions to be filled.

For years I have heard the argument that as baby boomers retire and leave the workplace there will be a shortage of skilled and knowledgeable workers. I have never embraced this belief. I believe technology and automation will streamline job functions such that there will not be the same demand for workers.

Reasons for the Career Plateau

Once an individual acknowledges a plateau has occurred, they typically want to determine why it happened. This a common psychological process and there are a number of factors put forward to explain why employees may become plateaued. For example, organizations may actively plateau employees for either organizational or interpersonal reasons.

But plateaued employees may perceive they have plateaued because of the organization's negative assessment of their capabilities.

They may feel the organization feels they either lack the ability to work in higher-level jobs, or do not desire one. In truth, managers within organizations may consciously (or subconsciously) pigeonhole employees: some are competent and willing to move up the corporate ladder and some are not.

An organization's assessment of an individual, whether it is accurate or not, may be an antecedent condition that the employee believes created his or her plateaued state. This can fuel negative emotions of resentment, frustration, and anger.

Recall in Chapter 4 that I referenced how faulty performance management processes may contribute to complacency.

My research — bolstered by my experience — leads me to believe errors in how performance is measured do affect whether or not individuals are seen as candidates for additional opportunities. One of the most difficult aspects of managing others relates to the responsibility for delivering difficult or negative feedback about individual performance.

And because it is difficult, many managers avoid the task of providing honest feedback when an employee's performance is not measuring up. As a result, individuals assume they are meeting expectations, or maybe even exceeding them. These behaviours, beliefs and assumptions contribute to a disconnect between reality and perception.

In other words, I may regard myself as being a high performer who is being held back because my manager does not like me.

In reality, my manager may perceive my performance is below expectations, but he or she is not comfortable giving me the "bad news." Thus, I may get pigeon-holed at a particular level in the organization, or in a particular job function.

Unless I figure out how my performance may be contributing to my results, I might be plateaued in the same spot for quite some time.

Another situation which may cause individuals to feel their organization has caused their plateau is the narrowing employment pyramid.

Creating Your Career / Denise O'Brien

As mentioned in Chapter 2, the organizational structure of many organizations allows fewer and fewer employees to move up to higher management ranks.

What's more, downsizing has eliminated many middle-management layers of the pyramid.

As firms cut employees throughout the organization, the structure becomes flattened, creating even more competition than previously.

Since flattened organizational structures are a fact of organizational life for the foreseeable future, fewer higher-level jobs will exist at many firms. And these organizational constraints may effectively plateau employees.

An employee's personal preference may be offered as the reason they have been plateaued. This may have become more prevalent with the high number of dual-career couples in the workforce.

Some individuals explicitly state they do not want to be promoted, while others send ambiguous signals or place constraints on proposed promotions.

The typical male employee in the 1970s was a strongly committed "organization man" whose every desire focused on staying with the company for life and progressing at a sure and steady pace up the hierarchy.

Hardly any of those individuals chose to be plateaued. Today, few workers embody the "organization man." Men and women may choose for personal reasons — family or health in particular — to not seek additional responsibilities.

Also, an individual may not feel the added stress associated with a promotion is worth what they may have to give up in order to do the job, regardless of how much more income might accrue to them.

So, we are at an interesting point in history where individuals may be plateaued for organizational assessment, organizational constraint, or personal-choice reasons.

The Good News About Arriving at a Career Plateau

Plateaus are a time to digest new ideas. They provide an opportunity to sit back and enjoy a highly desirable stable, secure, and restful phase of the work-life journey.

There is no need to feel pressured to reach another point, even though many of us continue to push ourselves to do so. Plateaus allow for reflection and offer individuals time to regroup and plan the next phase of personal and professional growth.

Plateaus give individuals the chance to embrace new knowledge and integrate that knowledge into their functional repertoire. From a more pragmatic perspective, plateaus allow time to "de-stress" and also to take stock of, and reinforce, accomplishments.

Some employees may even hope for a plateau due to their inability to cope with the stress career mobility and progression impose on them.

In fact, some plateaued employees have reported a greater likelihood of staying with and being committed to their organization.

Plateaued employees are expected to invest less of themselves in the job and more in non-work activities.

According to compensatory theory, disappointments in one sphere of life tend in some way to be made up for in another sphere.

For example, if you feel as though you have achieved a plateau in your work and are feeling restless or unfilled, perhaps consider opportunities to volunteer to augment your paid work activities.

There are many benefits to be gained from getting involved in non-work activities including learning new skills, expanding your network and helping to affirm self-esteem.

Similarly, plateaued individuals have more time to spend with their families, friends, leisure interests, and part-time work activities.

Finally, arriving at a plateau is a milestone that can offer many opportunities.

It is a matter of perspective and being able to recognize a plateau for the fact you have arrived at a peak and there is no room to advance further in your current role, or perhaps even in your organization.

If you are feeling as though you might be at a plateau in your work-life, see Chapters 7 and 8 for suggestions to help you navigate this phase of your work-life journey.

Recap of Key Points

1. Being plateaued is not a state of failure. It simply means we have arrived at a point in our work where we feel as though further progression and growth is not possible, or no longer of interest, or satisfying.

2. There are at least two ways in which we can feel plateaued in our work-life: we may feel as though there is nothing left to learn or feel challenged about in the work we are doing, indicating we have arrived at a functional plateau. Or, we may feel as though we are at an organizational plateau because, in the hierarchy, we have attained the highest position possible.

3. Most of us will arrive at multiple plateaus over the course of our working life.

4. Feeling plateaued is often mis-diagnosed as having a bad attitude, being unwilling to change, being difficult, having personal problems, or suffering from a mental health issue. In my experience, very few of us recognize when we have arrived at a career plateau.

5. There is no objective way to measure or predict how long it might take to arrive at a plateau in our work-life. There are too many variables—such as our personal motivation, our definition of success, the support our organization provides for learning and development etc.—to make it possible to estimate how long it might take to attain a plateau.

6. Plateaus have impacts upon job involvement, work satisfaction, turnover, and our personal well-being.

7. Being at a place in our work-life where we have arrived at — and achieved — a plateau is a milestone that can offer many opportunities. It is simply a matter of perspective and knowing how to recognize a milestone for what it is – a natural phase of one's work-life.

Best Advice and Tips to Navigate Plateaus

- Awareness: It is important to be sufficiently self-aware to notice you may be ready for a change – whether you have outgrown or lost interest in your current work, or perhaps you still enjoy the work itself, but your current workplace no longer affords you the opportunity to continue to advance or feel challenged.

- Recognition: When you arrive at a career plateau recognize it for what it is. Don't waste time or energy being angry or blaming yourself or anyone else. Recognize plateaus are a natural phase we all must learn to navigate.

- Function-Related Plateau: If you are feeling as though your current work is not a good fit —maybe you are bored, no longer feel challenged, or perhaps you are not passionate about it—figure out what you want to do about it. Here are a few suggestions to get you started.

    o Ask your manager to give you additional work.

    o If your work no longer feels like a good fit figure out what else you might like to do. You don't have to know with certainty, but at least identify other work that is more appealing to you. Seek information about work that is of interest. For example, qualifications, experience, and educational requirements are a good place to start.

- If your workplace is large enough, perhaps there are opportunities in other areas or departments which might be a better fit.

- Ask for additional learning opportunities to augment your skills and competencies, such as attending conferences or professional networking events or courses

- Organizational plateau: If you are feeling as though there is no room for growth and advancement in your current organization it is time to explore other options. Here are a few suggestions to get you started:

    - Networking: Reach out to your professional network and contacts to learn about other opportunities. Professional networking groups are an excellent way to hear about companies in your field that are looking for your skills, knowledge, qualifications etc.

    - Stay positive: While you explore external opportunities, keep yourself positive and engaged at work. Offer to mentor others. Be helpful.

    - Engage a professional coach: Sometimes we need assistance in keeping ourselves motivated and focused on moving forward. A professional coach can help!

Creating Your Career / Denise O'Brien

Chapter 7

The Exit Phase

> *Your objective in middle age is not to change your life. Your goal is to change how you experience your life!*
> **—Author Unknown**

The exit phase is one of my favourite career-related topics. I have always felt the chorus of the song, *The Gambler* by Don Schltiz summarizes this phase beautifully. The song was made famous in the 1970s by singer Kenny Rogers, who crooned: "You've got to know when to hold 'em, know when to fold 'em, know when to walk away and know when to run…"

Unfortunately, many of us do not heed this wisdom as we navigate our working life and thus we miss the signs we are heading towards — or are already in — the exit phase.

Compared to the other phases of our career, the exit phase gets the least amount of attention, even though it is a critical phase with significant implications for our life and well-being.

There are two ways we might make a permanent exit from work:

1. Voluntarily leaving, through resignation or retirement (we discuss retirement in Chapter 8).

2. Involuntarily leaving after being terminated or laid off.

Voluntary Exit

So, you've settled into work and have done your best to grow and maintain your career. You may even pride yourself on not having fallen victim to complacency and, although you may have hit a plateau or two, you have remained steadfast with the same organization.

At some point — and there is absolutely no way to predict or foresee when this may occur — you will reach an exit phase in your career.

Since it is estimated that the average adult will change jobs 12 times over the course of their working lives,[58] it is reasonable to assume we will reach the exit phase multiple times. Don't worry. You'll be fine.

There are some definite signs that it may be time to consider a change in your work or job or career. As you read the following list, I recommend you try to identify whether any of these issues might apply to you.

And consider if you might be at the point of needing to "hold 'em, or fold 'em" and whether it's time to "walk away or run."

---

[58] "Employee Tenure Summary," *US Bureau of Labor Statistics*, September 20, 2018

Creating Your Career / Denise O'Brien

Signs it May Be Time to Explore Other Options

Everyone has a bad day at work now and then. But if it feels as though there are more bad days than good ones, it may be time to leave your current work and choose to do something else. Below is a list of the possible signs.

- **You Dread Going to Work.** If you deeply hate your job, then you should absolutely start looking for other opportunities. Do you go to sleep every night dreading the next day of work? Losing sleep over work because you are worried is a sign something isn't right. Tune into these feelings. Open your eyes to feelings, thoughts, and events in your life that might alert you to the need to fold up.

- **You Procrastinate.** Everyone procrastinates on occasion, but if there is very little you find engaging about your day-to-day work, perhaps you should consider if your current position is really a good fit for you.
  While not every part of our work is going to be fascinating, interesting, or even enjoyable, there should be some tasks you enjoy doing,[59] and which feed your soul; otherwise you become one of the "walking dead." You might want to figuratively "walk away" because you likely do not have the energy to "run."

- **You Don't Feel Respected.** If you are not feeling respected by your manager it is most important to

---

[59] Michael Bungay Stanier, *Do More Great Work: Stop the Busywork and Start the Work That Matters* (Workman Publishing Company, Inc. New York, 2010)

address this with him or her. We teach people how to treat us and when we fail to call people on their treatment of us, it robs us of our dignity and erodes our self-worth.

- If you have attempted to address the disrespect with your manager and the treatment continues, this is a sign it is time to re-evaluate what's next for you. Don't stay working for a manager who does not treat you with respect.

- **Your Health Has Been Affected.** Are your sick days adding up, out of the blue? Are you taking as much time off as you can possibly get? Are you resorting to a few (or many) glasses of wine each night to get over a bad day at work? Are you working so many hours you have no time to exercise, eat healthily or get enough sleep?

No job is worth sacrificing your personal well-being to maintain. During my research one individual recognized it was time to explore other options because she felt burnt out. This feeling is definitely an indication that it's time to at least consider whether it is the work itself, your attitude about the work, or something else that is not the best fit for you.

- **You Are Aware of Constant Negativity.** Think about your most common conversations. Be wary of people with negative mindsets who are constantly complaining with a "glass half empty" mentality. These people do not attract positive people. Eventually negative people are surrounded by other negative people, which feeds even more negativity. It becomes a vicious cycle of negativity.

A job should bring more positive than negative energy into your life. Reflect on your communication style and the frequency with which you complain, gossip, or find fault with other people or your circumstances.

Are you constantly complaining about your coworkers, your workplace, or the work you do? If you notice you tend to be more negative than positive it is time to hold 'em and re-evaluate. It might be time to fold 'em.

- **You're Overqualified.** If you are in a job for which you are overqualified, stay on alert for positions which fit your skills, and which will likely feel more fulfilling than a job, which does not match your level of expertise. Are you feeling pigeon-holed in a position? The current work may be a stepping-stone to something you aspire to be doing. Do not delay. Explore other options. Follow your passion. Feeling stuck is a sign it is time to walk — or maybe run — away.

- **There is No Advancement Potential.** If you aspire to move up or advance in your profession, and your current organization does not have the capacity to offer opportunities for growth, then it is a sign you need to begin looking elsewhere and consider other options. Committing your time and energy to a company that will not support the progress of your career — or your own growth — is likely to leave you feeling dissatisfied and disappointed. When this occurs, consider your options. Weigh the pros and cons of leaving and make an informed decision to stay, or to go. Whatever you decide to do, feel good that you had the courage and wisdom to make a choice. Do not, I repeat DO NOT sit back and feel sorry for yourself or second-guess your decision.

- **Respect and Integrity Are Lacking**. If you have lost respect for your boss or the organization it is a good time to evaluate your options. One woman described it this way: "the leadership style didn't mesh with me. I didn't respect him." Hand in hand with respect is integrity.

  Does your boss have integrity? Does your workplace have integrity? If you answered "no," then this may be a huge red flag indicating it is time to explore "what's next" for yourself. So, take some time to explore external opportunities.

- **You Are in a Negative Work Environment.** A negative environment is toxic; if your co-workers are constantly complaining, and your boss is persistently unhappy, the probability of your own contentment is extremely low. Moreover, a pessimistic atmosphere can even kill the passion you have for your career choice.

  If you find yourself in a situation like this, it is likely time to run. However, wait long enough to check your own attitude because you may be carrying the infectious negativity virus. Moving to another workplace will not cure any negativity virus you may be carrying. "Wherever you go, there you are."

- **You Are Being Headhunted.** Are headhunters reaching out to you? If so, that is your green flag to explore other options. This might be the right opportunity to move on. This is definitely a time to assess whether walking away is right for you.

- **Organizational Culture.** If you crave a flexible, work-from-home environment, but you are feeling stuck in a traditional nine-to-five job, you may feel discontent no matter how much you like other aspects of your position. If you have tried unsuccessfully to negotiate work arrangements that better fit your preferences it is time to consider other opportunities, so you are not feeling stuck.

There is a high price to pay for our emotional well-being when we stay stuck too long.

Organizational culture may seem like an unimportant consideration but trust me, it will have significant implications on how satisfied and motivated you are at work. It is similar to being in a relationship with a person with whom you are just not compatible.

Of course, there will be a honeymoon phase, but over time incompatibility makes divorce almost inevitable.
Be tuned in to how well you fit with the organization and the work itself and consider when the time is right to walk away before it gets ugly.

- **You Are Fearful.** You should feel confident and comfortable enough at work to voice your opinion, share your thoughts, and speak up for yourself. If you are fearful at work, chances are you might be fearful about walking away. Fair enough. However, working in an environment of fear is not a healthy choice. I encourage you to actively explore other options and be open to opportunities.

- **Your Work Lacks Zest.** We spend too much time at work to not enjoy it. You shouldn't feel trapped on a path of work for which you do not feel passion, or interest.

If you have lost zest for your work, perhaps you have plateaued. Open your mind to other opportunities that do speak to you and start moving in a direction you genuinely feel passionate about.

Are you experiencing any of the signs that it may be time for you to hold 'em, fold 'em, walk away or run?

If yes, check out the last section in this chapter for advice and tips from people who have successfully navigated this phase of their career.

But first, let's examine the other avenue for entering the exit phase. It is much more absolute than voluntarily leaving the organization, as the decision to leave is beyond an individual's control.

Involuntary Exit

Call it what you want—being laid off or downsized, getting dismissed or fired, receiving your pink slip or your walking papers…losing your work or job hurts.

The research is very clear on this point: job loss is a major life stressor that places people at high risk for negative mental and physical outcomes. Some perceive job loss as a trauma or major loss event that induces psychological reactions similar to losing a loved one to death.

Documented negative outcomes include depression, anger, worry, and threats to identity, self-concept, and self-esteem. Other potential side-effects of job loss are loss of control and feelings of helplessness, which can make us feel unmotivated and unwilling to put forth much effort. In other words, losing one's job sucks!

Research indicates there are typical "psychological" cycles most people experience when they go through the loss of a job. Before I explain those, I invite you to read about what it's like to be a typical job loss "survivor."

Example:

> Shortly after being assigned to lead his company's finance department Martin expressed his displeasure with how the department had been previously operated. He felt there were too many layers of management and too many managers. To make a long story short, he asked his team of three directors to reduce the number of manager titles and, if possible, to eliminate those managerial positions.
>
> Daryl, a Financial Analyst had worked in the finance department for 12 years. He and Martin had not gotten off to a good start: Daryl felt Martin was not genuine and spoke like politician who was essentially spouting rhetoric. When Daryl listened to Martin speak, he felt his words did not hang together coherently. And Martin did not like to be questioned about his decisions. He seemed to perceive questions and feedback as challenges and defiance.
>
> As he settled into his role, Martin surrounded himself with employees who smiled, nodded, and went along with his commands. These employees would take gossip and hearsay back to Martin, which fuelled his contempt and anger.
>
> In the meantime, there was tension in the department because there was no trust. Fear was accelerating like a raging fire. It was quite ugly working with people who were figuratively throwing colleagues under the bus.

This style of leadership was not unique to the finance department but seemed to have taken hold in the organization. It became the company's predominant culture as many departments had fired managers in the past and continued to do so now.

Those most at risk of being let go were management staff members who asked questions, challenged decisions, or showed any form of resistance to their managers.

When Martin's administrative assistant emailed Daryl one Monday afternoon to arrange for Martin to meet with him later that afternoon at the end of regular work hours Daryl missed the email message because he was busy focused on an assignment.

Daryl noticed the email that evening He responded, apologizing for missing the email, and he asked whether Martin had any other time available to meet with him. Daryl felt the request was odd.

Martin had never made such a request before and Daryl was quite aware he was not one of Martin's favourite employees, and therefore he was not someone he would tend to meet with.

Also, he had given no reason for wanting to meet with Daryl, which seemed rather strange to him as well.

The two arranged to meet late the next morning in a meeting room, rather than Martin's office, which was also unusual.

Typically, Daryl would have felt some anxiety about an upcoming meeting scheduled for the next day with the department head.

However, Daryl recalls feeling calm, perhaps resigned to whatever was to come.

At the scheduled meeting time, Daryl left his desk with his computer on and the documents he was working on scattered across his desk.

Daryl walked down the hallway, opened the door and noticed Martin and one his directors sitting at the table.

Martin stated, "We're going in a different direction and I'm going to have to let you go." Daryl thinks he might have said something like, "okay." Martin mentioned the director had a letter for Daryl, and he left it to the director to finish up the meeting.

The meeting lasted three or four minutes.

As Daryl walked back down the hallway towards the elevator, he noticed a couple of male colleagues tuned into what was happening.

Having seen others being let go, Daryl knew the company ensured there were some strong guys at the ready "just in case" the employee became angry and out of control.

At some point, as Daryl walked down the hallway, someone handed him his coat and a few personal items, because he was not allowed back in to the department.

Daryl quietly left the building and went to his car. His heart felt too big for his chest.

He was devastated. He was afraid he wouldn't be able to handle the one-hour drive home because his mind was racing with confusion.

Nonetheless, Daryl recalls feeling some level of release almost as though – "the worst has happened and I'm still breathing."

As much as being let go had come as a surprise, it really was, on some level, what Daryl had been expecting. For example, approximately six months earlier he had taken his photos and certificates off his office wall and taken them home.

He had also removed many personal items from his desk because he did not want colleagues packing up his personal items to courier to his home.

Daryl had watched the termination of other competent colleagues and as much as he had hoped he was indispensable to the organization, he was realistic enough to recognize he was not.

Now what?

Daryl did very practical things like seek legal advice.

He reached out to a couple of colleagues to let them know he would not be available to fulfill on previously scheduled meeting commitments with them because he was no longer with the organization.

Every day he made lists of potential contacts, job opportunities and activities in which he could engage, as he tried to figure out the answer to the question "now what?"

In the meantime, Daryl felt physically sick. He recalls he was literally unable to eat for three days.

Over the next month or so he lost weight and slept very little. He was a shell of his former self.

Shortly after being let go, Daryl reached out to one former colleague, as he wanted to maintain the friendship. Daryl did not get a response to his email.

A little later Daryl sent a message to his "friend's" personal email address. No response was ever received. This was hard.

Not only had Daryl lost his work, but he had also lost a connection with someone he had thought was a good friend.

Only one former colleague ever reached out to Daryl. They met a couple of times for lunch but contact soon dwindled.

For at least eight months after being let go Daryl had nightmares and dreams that he was still working for the organization.

He would awaken in the morning exhausted, as though he had actually gone to work.

Daryl was going through the motions to move forward with his life during the day and reliving work every night. It felt like Post Traumatic Stress Disorder.

Eventually, Daryl became frustrated with himself for allowing his former work to fill his thoughts as he tried to sleep.

As thoughts of his former work entered his sleep Daryl learned to remind himself that, "It's a dream. It's not real. I am not giving this another thought."

This technique worked beautifully and over time Daryl rarely thought about his former employer while he slept.

Daryl recalls that when he had been terminated he felt his life was over. But he kept putting one foot in front of the other.

When he would feel sorry for himself, he would ask himself questions like, "is this how I want to be feeling?" and "what one small thing can I do right this minute to feel better?"

Eventually, Daryl's days got filled with other activities. He started his own business doing work he loves.

He put forth more effort to participate in professional associations.

He attends educational events and continues to challenge himself to take on things as "stretch" activities.

Daryl indicates his life is full.

From time to time Daryl will have reminders of his former employer, but they are passing positive thoughts, only.

Dealing with Job Loss

As you can see, being separated from one's job is tough, and many people experience grief much the same way they do when someone close to them dies.

The feeling of loss is not surprising since a significant part of your life goes away when you lose your job; many of us closely identify ourselves by what we do for a living.

What can make job loss so traumatic is the shattering blow it delivers to our self-esteem.

When you are let go from a position, for whatever reason, the underlying message you may receive is, "I'm a failure. I am just not good enough. No matter what the economic times, if I were any good they would have kept me."

Thus, losing one's job causes us to lose sight of who we are and even *why* we are, that is, our purpose in life.

It triggers many emotions — so much so that it can feel almost too overwhelming and, like Daryl, your heart may feel too big for your chest. In those moments, you might even feel as though life as you know it is over.

Whatever feelings you experience, they are natural responses and they are to be expected. And in truth, the life you have known has been changed. Don't worry. You will be fine.

You *can* successfully navigate job loss. If you lose a job — just like Daryl in the example above — you *can* survive and thrive.

Navigating Job Loss

I have come to understand that the best way to approach the loss of one's job is the same way we approach all other major changes in our lives, including painful losses, joyous events such as getting married, or becoming an empty nester. Even happy events are still changes that can trigger feelings of loss.

The most important thing about navigating personal change is to understand that the emotions you may be experiencing are to be expected as you process what has happened and adapt to your new "normal."

Although there are many theories to explain how humans adapt to change, there are two theories which I find have the greatest practical application here:

1. Elisabeth Kübler-Ross – Stages of Grief

When dealing with a major life event (both happy and sad events) most of us experience some version of the five traditional stages of grief.
We're all different, so we all experience them differently. **Elisabeth Kübler-Ross**, the psychiatrist who identified these stages, said we don't necessarily experienced them in a linear fashion, and some people might not experience them at all. They're just broad, common stages people go through when grieving a death, a divorce or the loss of a job.

Recognizing where you are is extremely useful. It is a way to remind ourselves we are human and our are feelings are okay.

Five Stages of Grief - Elisabeth Kübler-Ross

STAGE	MEANING
1 - **Denial**	***Denial*** is a conscious or unconscious refusal to accept facts, information, reality, etc., relating to the situation at hand. It's a perfectly natural defence mechanism . For example, you might pretend that losing your job is no big deal. But you may be denying feelings such as hurt, disappointment, or worthlessness. Essentially, we protect ourselves from experiencing pain when we are in the Denial phase. This can be helpful for a short time to protect ourselves, however some people can become locked in this stage. Remaining in Denial is not wise as it will affect our health and well-being in the long term.

2 - **Anger**   As we process the event, we move away from Denial and might naturally move to the ***Anger*** stage. Anger can manifest in different ways. For example, people dealing with emotional upset can be angry with themselves, and/or others, especially those close to them. It is helpful to recognize that feelings of anger are good—and to be expected. However, if we remain too long in this stage we can become our own worst enemy, expending negative energy in unproductive, often destructive ways.

3 - **Bargaining** Traditionally the ***Bargaining*** stage for people facing death can involve attempting to bargain with whatever God they believe. People facing less serious trauma can bargain or seek to negotiate with themselves and others. For example, in the situation described earlier involving Daryl, we noted he wanted to remain friends with a former co-worker. This might be Daryl's attempt to "negotiate" and maintain some connectedness to the workplace he had involuntarily left behind.

When he received no response from his attempts, Daryl faced yet another tough loss. Bargaining rarely provides a sustainable solution. Rather, Bargaining is a short-term "idea" in which we grasp at straws trying to regain some sense of normalcy and remain connected to what we've lost. I regard the Bargaining phase as our attempt to find ways to make it easier to accept what has happened.

4 - **Depression**   ***Depression*** is also referred to as "preparatory grieving." In a way it's the dress rehearsal for the "aftermath" of what is happening, although this stage can mean different things to different people. It essentially represents an acceptance of what's happening, but with emotional attachment.

It's natural to feel sadness, regret, fear, uncertainty, etc., when something dramatic happens in our lives. It shows we have begun to accept reality. Similar to the stages of Denial and Anger, it's important to avoid staying too long in the Depression stage as it can be debilitating. Individuals navigate grief and setbacks according to their own unique schedule. I believe [60] there are no prescribed timelines to heal from setbacks.

5 - **Acceptance** *Acceptance* can look and feel different for each individual although, broadly speaking, it is an indication that a person is at least somewhat emotionally detached from what has happened, and feeling a little more objective about it. Kübler-Ross found in her work that people who are dying tend to enter this stage a long time before the people they leave behind, who must necessarily pass through their own stages of dealing with the grief. With regard to job loss, at some point we must accept we no longer have the job we had before.

As Kübler-Ross's work tells us, the grieving process does not happen in an organized and straightforward fashion. It follows no timelines.

For example, you might feel good about things one day, as though you have moved to the acceptance stage, but later regress to feeling anger or a sense of depression.

Again, it is all perfectly normal.

Let me illustrate how navigating the grieving process sometimes works through the story one woman, who I will call Amanda, shared with me about her experience:

---

[60] Elisabeth Kübler-Ross, *On Death and Dying*, (MacMillan New, York, 1969).

Creating Your Career / Denise O'Brien

> *"I literally cried all the way home. I cried all night and my husband said, 'What on earth? You know what you're going to do. You're going to start your own business. You've known this has been coming. What's going on?' I said, 'Don't stop me I just have to do this …'And that loss was such an eye-opener for me to understand the lack of control that I had in the situation because I never knew what that pain felt like … It's being out of control.*
>
> *"I was going through the grieving process, because I loved my job. You know, I'd get up in the morning and be fine when I was going all day but as soon as my head hit the pillow at night, the last thought was "I don't have a job." First thought in the morning was, 'I don't have a job.'"*

During the day, her mind and body were occupied doing tasks and solving other day-to-day issues.

Amanda did not give much thought to losing her job.

Perhaps she was in the acceptance stage during the day, but at night her mind regressed to other stages of grief, such as anger or bargaining.

Think back to Daryl's example of job loss. You will recall his sleep was consumed with thoughts of his former job to the extent that as he slept he regressed to the denial, anger or bargaining stages.

Eventually, Daryl moved to the acceptance stage both during his sleeping and waking hours.

It takes time but keep in mind, "this too shall pass."

2. William Bridges – Phases of Transition

Another practical change model which I use to assist people with the successful navigation of job loss is one put forward by William Bridges.

During his life, Bridges wrote extensively on change and transition.

In his book, *Transitions: Making Sense of Life's Changes,* Bridges discusses strategies for navigating "the difficult, painful and confusing times" in life.[61]

Essentially, Bridges proposes that "change" is an event. For instance, Daryl was advised his services were no longer required. That was a traumatic *event* – which is the change.

However, Bridges describes the way in which Daryl came to terms with, and learned to accept that his previous job was gone from his life, as a psychological transition.

The change is an event to which one can attach a specific time.

For example, perhaps Daryl's former boss advised him at 10:30 in the morning that his employment was terminated.

The emotional aftermath of that change event was yet to be experienced or felt by Daryl.

Like Kübler-Ross, Bridges proposes that changes are navigated in stages as part of a bigger process in which it is not possible to predict how long it will take to psychologically transition to the new reality.

---

[61] William Bridges, *Transitions: Making Sense of Life's Changes*, 2nd Edition, (Ca Capo Lifelong Books, Boston, 2011).

Although the length of time it takes to navigate the transition is situational and varies from person to person, Bridges argues that the psychological transition through change events occurs over three phases.

One of the most important points I hope you take away from this chapter is that job loss is not the end of your life.

It can be excruciatingly painful; however it is only the end of one aspect of your life.

Trust me, you are perfectly capable of not only surviving from the loss, but actually *thriving*.

I cannot tell you how often I have spoken with people who lost their jobs only to end up much better off as a result.

While researching for this book I had the pleasure to speak with numerous job loss survivors.

I have included some of the sage wisdom from these survivors at the end of this chapter, in the section "Best Advice and Tips to Navigate the Exit Phase."

PHASE	WHAT IT LOOKS LIKE
Ending	***Ending*** occurs when we disengage from the old ways of doing things and let go of who we were in that situation. As we saw with Amanda, she seemed able to let go of her former job after some crying and feeling sorry for herself. **Tips to navigate ending;** • Decide what in your life/work is over, and what isn't • Figure out what you are really losing. In most cases, not everything is lost (although it might feel

Creating Your Career / Denise O'Brien

	like it is) • Actively seek information by asking questions, and researching the answers to your questions • Recognize and accept it feels painful and you are mourning the loss • Identify symbolic pieces of the past to take with you such as photos and keepsakes • Deal with one thing at a time rather than choosing to make radical and perhaps unnecessary changes – give yourself time to come to terms with what's happened. **Ask yourself** • What is ending? • What am I losing in this change? • What is going to be better? • What are the opportunities now open to me? • What assumptions am I making? • What are the facts • Who can I ask for help? In the ending phase what looks like resistance is really doubt, fear, uncertainty etc. Don't worry. You will be fine.
Neutral Zone	*The Neutral Zone* is a confusing, in-between state, when we are not who and where we were, but we are not yet who and where we are going to be, either. For example, when Daryl lost his job, he was feeling lost because what he had known in life was over. Even as he moved forward, he was drawn back into work during his sleeping hours. In the neutral zone, we can feel like victims. This is a necessary state of being for it is during this time that your own inner transformation is taking place. In other words, it is perfectly normal. Lean into it with courage. Don't worry. You will be fine. **Tips to navigate the neutral zone:** • Try to identify what you do have control over and take action with those things • Try to be realistic and not too hard on yourself

	- Identify some realistic goals for yourself
- Ask questions. Seek information.
- Create temporary structures to get you through the "wilderness." For example, get a membership to a gym and commit to getting up at your usual time and go to the gym to workout. Connect with friends and meet for lunch. Commit to taking care of household projects you have been ignoring for a while. Humans are creatures of habit. During this time, create some new habits for yourself.
- Accept this is a normal part of the psychological transition
- Remember that "this too shall pass. You will be fine."
The New Beginning	*The New Beginning* occurs as we grow familiar with and accept (although not necessarily like) the new reality change brings. In this final phase of transition, we begin to identify with the situation we are in. For example, Daryl came to terms with his job loss and eventually his former employment became a distant and positive memory. Beginnings come only after we have let go of the old way and have spent some time in the chaos of the neutral zone. So, do not think you will skip the neutral zone. You will feel energized by new beginnings, especially after the dark, confusing, discouraging days in the neutral zone. **Tips to navigate a successful new beginning:** - Be open to shifts and corrections in your plan.
- Try to keep other, unrelated changes to a minimum. In other words, as much as possible, avoid adding other major life changes to your plate.
- Focus your attention on what's positive in your life, as it fuels your enthusiasm and energy.
- Celebrate your "new" reality.

Recap of Key Points

1. The exit phase of our career is inevitable. Since it is estimated that the average adult will change his or her job position approximately 12 times during their working life, it is reasonable to expect we will reach the exit phase multiple times during our career.

2. I propose that the exit phase happens in one of two ways: voluntarily or involuntarily. Both can be extremely difficult changes to navigate.

3. Remember the Gambler analogy. There are many signs to help us know it might be time to "hold 'em," "fold 'em," "walk away," or "run" from our current work, job, or career. Tune in to the signs like it *really* matters — because it does!

4. Job loss is a trauma or major loss event which induces psychological reactions similar to losing a loved one to death or terminal illness. Documented negative outcomes include depression, anger, worry, and threats to identity, self-concept, and self-esteem.

5. Job loss does not mean life is over. Rather, one part of your life has changed. This too shall pass.

6. Two models of change are offered in this chapter – Elisabeth Kübler-Ross's Five Stages of Grief and William Bridges's Change and Transition model. Both offer practical insight about the stages or phases of getting through a change.

7. I cannot stress enough that negative emotional responses are perfectly normal after suffering a loss. Learning to recognize the various phases is helpful because it helps affirm that we're okay. We feel emotionally maimed by the event, which is to be expected. However, we must put it in perspective and continue to move forward.

8. Don't worry. You will be fine.

Best Advice, Tips to Navigate the Exit Phase

- Recognize that leaving work and careers is inevitable. Stay tuned into the signs it may be time to consider other options.

- Live within your means. Assume there is no Plan B and have some money set aside. This will give you security in case — God forbid — you find yourself unemployed.

- Don't put up with people who don't respect you.

- Job loss is tough, give yourself time to mourn the loss — but to move forward you have to let it go.

- Create new habits and routines.

- Stay connected to others.

- Take care of yourself with balanced habits of healthy eating, exercise and sleep.

Creating Your Career / Denise O'Brien

Chapter 8

Retirement

> ***Things which matter most must never be at the mercy of things which matter least.***
> **— Johann Goethe**

Some of you reading this book may be in the very early stages of your working life and nowhere close to retirement. I completely understand this feeling because I, too, recall thinking, "retirement is the least of my worries," and "I will get around to it one day." Thinking about and planning for retirement was not something to which I gave much thought. In hindsight, this was unwise.

However, in fairness, trying to balance the demands of work and family and life can be overwhelming to the extent that it feels as though there are not enough hours in the day or week or month or even year to plan for a retirement that seems so far off into the future.

Regardless of which phase of your work you are currently experiencing, I encourage you to refrain from burying your head in the sand about the issue of your retirement.

It is an inevitable stage of your working life and it is helpful to be thinking about, and informing yourself about, what lies ahead so you can better navigate the challenges ahead.

Retirement. The word conjures up wonderful visions of being on vacation all the time. Sleeping late. Taking trips. Finally having enough time to indulge in whatever hobby or interest catches your fancy.

If you are wise and conscientious, you will have saved for retirement in a variety of ways, working and waiting until the day when you decide it is time, and you are ready to "fold 'em" and leave full-time work behind.

Prior to 2006, in Canada, mandatory retirement went hand-in-hand with turning 65-years of age.

However, jurisdictions across the country changed retirement legislation to make it illegal for employers to impose mandatory retirement: it had come to be regarded as age discrimination.

Before 2006, however, once you arrived at your 65th birthday (unless you were self-employed) your employment typically ceased, whether you would have preferred to stay working, or not.

I recall conversations with individuals in the days before the legislation was passed. They expressed gratitude for the fact that they were required to retire upon turning 65 because there was no decision for them to make about the subject.

Throughout their working life, they had known that upon turning 65 years of age they would need to retire. They worked and planned accordingly.

However, now that the rules have changed and there is no mandatory retirement age, some people talk about how work feels "never ending" and they are forced to deliberate over whether to leave their job or stay.

Many people continue to work well beyond their 65th birthday because they cannot afford to retire, and they feel "stuck."

As mentioned in the previous chapter, it's been my experience that few of us are good at "knowing when to hold 'em, fold 'em, walk away or run."

We stay in workplaces too long, and for the wrong reasons.

My point is, think about and plan for retirement even though there is no mandatory retirement age. There will come a point in your working life when you really need to retire.

It's a Dog's Life

I believe that when we are in our 50s and 60's each year of work is measured as a "dog year." For anyone unfamiliar with the concept, we know that every year of a dog's life is equivalent to seven years of a human being's life.

Thus, dogs age much faster than people, which means we end up outliving our beloved dogs. I have come to the conclusion that as we leave our 20s, 30s, and 40s behind and head into our 50s each day of work can be measured in dog years.

For example:

- A single day can begin to feel seven times longer than it used to;

- Learning something new can take seven times longer and feel seven times harder than previously;

- We can become seven times more stubborn and resistant to anything new than we were when we were younger;

- We leave work at the end of the day feeling seven times more tired and

- It takes 7x times longer to recover from workdays.

Keep in mind that by the time the average adult moves into their 50s they may have been working for 20 or 30 years.

Reasons for Retirement

Not everybody retires by choice. Some people are forced to do so because of illness or physical problems, which prevent them from continuing in their careers.

Others may be laid off or downsized. Sometimes these forced or early retirements result in a financial burden. Be mindful of advice offered earlier in this book and plan accordingly.

Forced retirement feels very much like any other form of "involuntary" job loss and if that happens to you, you are likely to experience emotional reactions similar to those mentioned in Chapter 7.

But even if you do retire by choice, and even if you have enough money coming in to support yourself, you could find that retirement isn't all you thought it would be.

Going from working a full-time job to having nowhere specific you "have" to be each day sounds fantastic, but some retirees end up feeling bored and unproductive. After years of a structured schedule, the hours can seem endless and this has consequences for our personal well-being.

For example, according to research by the Canadian Coalition for Seniors' Mental Health[62] it is estimated **as many as 10% of Canadians** suffer from depression after retirement.

That figure leaps as high as 40% when it comes to retirees who live in an institution, such as a nursing home.

There are many reasons why depression after retirement is so prevalent. When we stop working, many of us feel a loss of purpose or even identity. We suddenly have a lot of extra time on our hands and many people struggle to fill that time in a meaningful way. Social lives that revolve around work are suddenly taken away from us and we can become more isolated.

Example:

Linda started working at part-time jobs during high school and upon graduation from university she

---

[62] "Depression in Older Adults: A Guide for Seniors and their Families," *Canadian Coalition for Seniors' Mental Health*.

worked full-time until she retired at 60 years of age when she realized she was not enjoying her work anymore.

She had felt hesitant about retirement because it meant spending more time at home with her husband, John. He had retired three years earlier and Linda had watched his energy and enthusiasm for life diminish more every year.

Although they enjoyed spending time with their three adult children and five grandchildren, Linda found that John's interest in them was waning. Linda encouraged him to take up some hobbies—perhaps play golf, or maybe volunteer on some community projects.

John dismissed all of Linda's suggestions and spent more time watching television and reading the news online. She watched John's zest for life diminish, and it frightened her to think about how they were ever going to endure the years ahead.

As Linda watched her husband become more sedentary in retirement it brought her to the realization that she absolutely did not want to retire and watch television or spend her days surfing the internet.

So, approximately two years before she actually retired Linda started making plans for the next chapter of her life.

She identified projects she wanted to tackle and made it a point to get more involved in local activities. She joined the recreation centre in her town and took whatever interesting classes they offered around her work schedule. As she attended classes, Linda met other women her age with whom she shared common interests.

Creating Your Career / Denise O'Brien

Retirement Planning Basics:

The Needs of Men and Women are Different

The questions most people think about before retirement are "How much money will I need?" and "Am I saving enough?"

While I wholeheartedly agree financial security is certainly critical, I believe a well-rounded approach to retirement planning is more preferable. In particular, people also need to stockpile their emotional reserves.

The truth is, too few people consider the psychological adjustments that accompany this stage of life: you will need to cope with the loss of your career identity, replace the support networks that had been available to you through work, find new and engaging ways to stay active and most importantly navigate how to spend more time than ever before with your spouse.

Recall that Linda recognized that retirement meant spending more time at home with a spouse with whom she had very little in common. This scenario is not unique to Linda and her husband: it is a reality all of us must face because retirement requires both partners to adjust to new circumstances.

During the course of my research, and the many conversations I enjoyed with people, I heard examples of how men and women are wired differently and thus adapt differently to retirement. For instance, Joyce put it this way,

"I think men just feel lost if they don't have something that they can get into. You know, like my husband, for the first time in his life he's got friendships right now. A lot of it sort of came out of church and golf. A man has to have an activity to have a friend.

"Women just have friends – they don't need to be doing anything. You know, we just get together, we just enjoy talking. We are open with each other and vulnerable. But men have to be doing something, some sort of activity to make them want to congregate and do something. Men when they communicate it's, one-upmanship, like they don't like to be in the position of asking for advice."

So, while it might seem like retirement is a time to take it easy and devote yourself to gardening, golfing, and napping, optimal well-being requires us to stay engaged—with personal interests as well as with other people.

To help you to build a well-rounded reserve of all you will need in retirement I offer the following:

Consider Part-Time Work

Some people resist retirement because they feel as though it means their working life is completely over. It can feel scary to leave behind what you have known for much of your adult life. I absolutely encourage people to be thinking about retirement as an opportunity to explore other options, including the idea of part-time work. There are many benefits to continuing in the workforce in some capacity, assuming you're able to do so.

Making money and bolstering your financial situation is one of them—many people find that their savings do not go as far as they thought they would, due to the rising cost of living. Even if you are in a good place financially, you could

Creating Your Career / Denise O'Brien

use the money to pay off debt, save for an extended vacation, or invest in some home improvements.

Having a regular schedule and interacting with different people on a daily basis can also help maintain your emotional and mental health.

In some companies, transitioning to part-time or flextime is an option for people in their retirement years. Maybe just cutting back on working hours is a good compromise between continuing those 60-hour work weeks and fully retiring.

Many retirees take part-time jobs, either related to their previous careers or in an entirely different field. The senior citizen bagging groceries may seem like a cliché, but this is an example of a relatively low-stress job, which can work well for retirees. Depending on how many hours you're working, how much money you make, and the makeup of your retirement income, you may be able to continue to draw a pension while you work.

I recall conducting an exit interview with a gentleman as he was leaving full-time employment and I asked, "what's next?" He immediately responded, "I'm off to Walmart to put in my application to be a Greeter." He knew he needed to "fold 'em" and leave behind the physically and cognitively demanding work he had been doing for many years.

However, he also loved interacting with people, and he recognized the structure of a job as a Greeter would give him that opportunity. At least he wanted to give it a shot! Another woman told me she knew it was time to leave her fulltime work in the accounting sector, but she was not ready to stay home.

Her husband had passed away a few years earlier, her children were grown and raising their own families and she had worked since she was a teenager. It seemed scary to think about not having a job.

So, she went to the local community centre and applied for a part-time job working in the canteen. The hours were flexible, the work itself was not physically or cognitively demanding and she had opportunities to stay engaged with others.

The opportunity to work part-time allowed these individuals to ease into retirement – gradually, and at a comfortable pace.

Share Your Knowledge

Even if teaching, consulting or mentoring were not your profession you can take these activities up after you retire. You don't necessarily have to teach children (although if you're interested in a second career, it's a possibility), but you might certainly be interested in teaching and mentoring other adults around the topic of what you have learned in the years spent in your chosen industry.

Some colleges and technical schools employ people who have a lot of real-world experience to teach continuing education programs. Many companies also employ consultants, or coaches, or bring in speakers to share their knowledge with their employees.

You might also consider teaching other skills you have acquired which do not necessarily have anything to do with your career. Local community schools hold classes in everything from foreign languages to horseback riding.

If you've long been quilting, growing a vegetable garden or crafting wooden children's toys, you might get opportunities to teach people who are interested in learning a skill you've already mastered.

There is nothing more rewarding than sharing your knowledge to help others, and it keeps us mentally stimulated, as well.

Continue Learning

You may have heard that it's never too late to go back to school but have never really considered it for yourself.

If you have spent all of your adult life working full-time and raising children, there may not have been time to even think about pursuing additional degrees or even getting a college degree at all. But plenty of senior citizens are earning undergraduate or graduate degrees.

Continuing your education keeps your mind sharp and active. And it could mean the opportunity to learn more about a lifelong passion, or start on another career.

With expanding technologies, online instruction has grown in popularity and availability. Pretty much anything you can think to study is accessible online.

One caution, though, is this: do not take any courses unless you are passionate about the topic.

Take courses that sincerely interest you, and for the pure joy of learning. If you find you are not interested in a topic – let it go. Do not waste precious time and energy on topics which are not feeding you.

If you take courses, do not put pressure on yourself to be a star student. Keep in mind your purpose is not to attain the top mark in the class (unless that is the purpose that feeds your soul), rather it is for the pure joy of learning.

Start a Hobby

Ideally, you will start at least some hobbies long before you retire. Avoid being like many of us who have skills or hobbies we wish we had picked up but never did. Now is your chance. Want to learn how to play the piano? Become a master gardener? Ballroom dance? Many of these hobbies can be learned in classes offered online or in-person through local colleges and not-for-profit groups. Depending on the type of class you take and how often it's offered, these seminars are usually inexpensive. And many groups offer seminars specifically for senior citizens. You can also find a "how-to" video on YouTube for pretty much any craft or hobby you want to learn.

Volunteer

I cannot emphasize enough the value of volunteering – both to you as the volunteer and the organizations that are the recipients of your generosity. Volunteering and joining community groups can help older adults meet new people with similar interests and values which may lead to new friendships or help rekindle old ones.

Although I believe that at all points in our lives we should be doing at least some volunteering, and giving back to our community, I recognize it can be a struggle to find time when we're working fulltime, and juggling the demands of family and life. However, retirement can be the perfect time to perform community service through volunteering. There are so many reasons why we should volunteer. It can help you:

Gain a sense of self and purpose. After retirement, it may be difficult to feel purposeful and connected to others and the community. However, volunteering can lead to a sense of accomplishment and belonging.

Many people may argue they don't have the time or energy to participate, yet I've heard from many that volunteering for as little as one hour a week can result in cognitive and emotional benefits.

For example, my neighbour turned 97 years old this year and she continues to volunteer to sew items for community organizations. She explained to me that it "keeps her sharp." All of these factors combined lead to increased self-esteem and wellness.

- **Develop new skills.** There are many ways for retirees to become involved in their community. It's never too late to learn something new and step outside your comfort zone. Even if mobility is an issue, as is the case with my 97-year old neighbour, there are lots of ways to make a difference. Here are a few examples:

    o   Sew, quilt, or in some way share your skills

    o   Sponsor a local family in need

    o   Create a neighbourhood lending library

    o   Donate old towels or blankets to the animal shelter

    o   Volunteer with the local hospital auxiliary

    o   Participate in church, synagogue, or mosque activities

- **Reduce the risk of dementia.** A study led by a University of Calgary[63] professor found people who regularly volunteered at least one hour a week were 2.44 times less likely to develop dementia than seniors who did not. The study found it was important the volunteer activity benefitted people who were not part of participants' core family. For example, it was best if they helped out at a church, a school, a library, a homeless shelter or a charitable organization.

Get Involved in Politics

Casting your vote when election time rolls around is just the tip of the iceberg when it comes to participating in the political process.

Think back to the last time you walked into a polling place — did the workers there have something in common? There's a good chance many of them were senior citizens. Working the polls is an easy way to play a part in the political process.

You doubtless have strong opinions about who should be chosen to represent you, and you state those opinions when you vote, but if you like a specific candidate, call his or her local office and ask how you can help him or her get elected.

You could find yourself making phone calls to potential voters, stuffing envelopes or coordinating fundraisers and rallies. It doesn't matter whether you're working for someone running for local or national office; they all need volunteer help to get there.

---

[63] Yannick Griep et al, "Can Volunteering in Later Life Reduce the Risk of Dementia? A 5-year longitudinal study among volunteering and non-volunteering retired seniors." *Public Library of Science (PLOS One)*

If you don't want to campaign for a particular candidate, consider the issues that most affect you and the pieces of legislation on which your local and national representatives could vote. There are no doubt countless grassroots and special interest groups devoted to an issue you care. They work to get politicians interested in their cause and provide legislative support, and they need volunteers.

During my research one woman, who I'll call Ellen, told me she felt completely lost after her employment ceased when her company went bankrupt. In her early 50s at the time, she felt too young to even consider retirement. Although she received a generous pension from her former company, Ellen thought about things she'd always wanted to do – including running for a political office. Ellen drew on her skills, competencies, knowledge, and network of contacts and successfully won the political seat she'd sought. She went on to enjoy many years in political office.

Stay Active

Despite all of the things you could be doing, it's easy to get into a rut when you're retired—like John in the example shared earlier in the chapter—especially if you live alone. Sitting around the house is bad for your mental and your physical health. If you're the only person who has retired in your circle of friends, you may find that you don't have as much in common with them. Plus, retirees in cold climates often move to warmer parts, so even your retired friends might disappear for months at a time. You may have to seek out new friends, and the community seniors' centre is a good place to start. Seniors' centres offer recreational and social opportunities. They hold luncheons and dances and organize trips to historical sites and shopping destinations. Seniors' centres also have clubs or groups for different interests, such as book clubs.

Creating Your Career / Denise O'Brien

I heard a radio interview one day with Dick Van Dyke, an actor popular in the 1960s and 1970s. At the time, I believe Mr. Van Dyke was 89 years old. The host asked what his secret for living a long life was. Mr. Van Dyke said "just keep moving. Put one foot in front of the other. Don't stop moving." I absolutely concur with this advice. And, even if we have limited physical mobility, we can still keep our minds active.

Travel

Finally, if you ask most people what they look forward to about retirement, the ability to travel is often high on the list. Retirees are seen as people with endless amounts of free time and few attachments to keep them from spending months away from home. If you have the money to travel, and the desire, why not go for it?

You could also combine work and play. Several companies organize volunteer vacations—you travel to a destination and spend part of your time helping to build homes in impoverished areas or cleaning up national parks. Some retirees teach English or other subjects in foreign countries to offset their expenses.

During my research, one woman told me that as she started planning for retirement she began looking for opportunities to become a tour guide for seniors groups in exotic places around the globe. As the guide, her travel expenses would be covered, and she could learn lots and meet many new people. The point is, there are lots of ways to make retirement an amazing chapter in our full lives. Some (like running for a political office) require pre-planning and a lot of hard work but others are simple: "just keep moving. Put one foot in front of the other. Don't stop moving."

Creating Your Career / Denise O'Brien

	Pre-Retirement Planning CHECKLIST	Response	
	This checklist identifies important considerations for building a reserve to sustain a healthy retirement	Yes	No
1	I have been setting aside money to be able to financially survive during my retirement years.		
2.	I have consulted a financial planner to get independent advice about my retirement plan.		
3	I stay informed and active in my community.		
4.	I have good friends with whom I stay actively connected.		
5.	I stay physically active through exercise and other activities.		
6.	I currently have some hobbies.		
7.	I've made a list of interests and hobbies I plan to pursue in my retirement.		
8.	I've made a "bucket list" of places I want to visit when I retire.		
9.	I volunteer my time.		
10.	I've made a list of not-for-profit organizations for which to volunteer to support their efforts.		
11.	I always put myself out to meet new people.		
12	I challenge myself to learn something new every day, week, month or year.		
13.	I have identified a course I really want to take for the pure joy of learning.		
14.	I take care of myself by consuming healthy amounts of food and alcohol.		
15.	I have a strong network for social and emotional support		
Total			
Tabulating your results: Add up your responses in the "Yes" and No" columns. Congratulations for all your "Yes" responses! If you have responded "No" to any questions I encourage you to find ways to strengthen your capacity in this regard. Trust me, it will make retirement a whole lot easier.			

Recap of Key Points

1. Retirement is an inevitable stage of your working life. Be proactive in thinking about it and informing yourself about what lies ahead.

2. I believe that when we are in our 50s each year of work is measured as a "dog year." If you are feeling work is seven times more complicated, frustrating etc., it might be time to consider retirement.

3. Many people regard retirement planning as an exercise for planning their finances. Research indicates financial planning is essential, but it is also important to build up your emotional reserves, as well.

4. In general, women and men transition to retirement differently.

5. The truth is, retirement represents the end of one's work-life, which can be emotionally difficult.

6. There are many ways to ease into retirement, including working part-time, doing some volunteer work, working on some personal development projects, sharing your knowledge, travelling, becoming politically active, and pursuing some hobbies and interests.

Creating Your Career / Denise O'Brien

Best Advice and Tips to Navigate Retirement

Planning: Absolutely begin planning for retirement as early as possible. In fact, some have suggested to me that the time to begin planning for retirement is as soon as you enter the workforce. Yikes! If you are like me, you are not that organized. Nonetheless, start as early as you can to think about — and plan for — the inevitable.

- Financial planning – every week or month put aside at least some portion of your income for your retirement.

- Location – be thinking about where you would like to be living when you retire. For instance, if you tend to have health or mobility issues you most likely want to live in areas that are accessible to medical facilities. If you love to golf or attend plays and the theatre, then living within a comfortable distance to these activity venues may be preferable. Do you want to live closer to family members?

- Living arrangements: plan for your living needs. Do you want to have a yard with grass to cut or do you prefer to live in a maintenance-free unit. How much physical space will you need?

- Relationships: Don't wait until you retire to nurture relationships. Stay connected to others because they will be essential in retirement when you have more time on your hands. What's more, don't limit your social connections to your children and grandchildren. They are often busy with their own lives and you need to safeguard against making your life revolve around them.

- Interests and Hobbies: Long before you retire, invest time and energy in developing hobbies and leisure activities.

One day I had a conversation with a 67-year old gentleman, whom I'll refer to as Randy. He told me he was looking forward to retirement because he had bought himself a boat and he planned to fish every day.

I asked Randy how long it had been since he last went fishing to which he responded, "oh, it's been years." I knew in that moment that fishing was unlikely to hold much interest for Randy during his retirement, because interests are not something we switch on when we are 67 years of age.

If Randy had truly been interested in, and passionate about, fishing he would likely have been doing even a bit of fishing over the years.

As it turned out, after Randy retired he took his boat out fishing only a few times before he sold it. The point is this: interests and hobbies need to be nourished with actual activity.

Saying "I'm interested in learning something new," isn't the same as actually learning something new. Talk is cheap and will not sustain you in your retirement.

Final Thoughts …

My deepest hope is that you've found useful nuggets of information and advice in this book to help you on your work-life journey. In this last section, I offer some insights that have served me well in all aspects of my life:

Be Present. When I was growing up my Father used to say: "If you only do one thing, do it well." In other words, focus your energy on one thing at a time.

Apply yourself to the best of your abilities and take pride in whatever you tackle.

No matter what you do or where you go, show up and be present. Another term often used to describe presence is "mindfulness."

Too often, we try to do many things at once, or we pack our days with more tasks than is realistic; we end up rushing from one thing to the next. In these situations, we mostly aren't doing anything particularly well.

We show up at meetings and events, and focus only part of our energy on the task at hand. We end up checking our smartphone or thinking about our "to-do list."

We show up at work, and then spend much of the day thinking about, and worrying about, our personal life. And, when we're at home, we expend precious time and energy focused on, and obsessing over, work stuff.

As an adult, I have come to appreciate my Father's advice and I make it my practice to be fully present in everything I do.

Let me qualify this with an admission that I'm human and when I'm tired or grumpy or feeling overwhelmed I do not always succeed in being fully present in everything. However – I work hard at it because it feels so much better than doing things in a half-hearted or rushed fashion.

Choosing to be fully present requires conscious effort.

If you need some help learning how to be fully present I recommend a wonderful book written by Dr. Richard Carlson: *Don't Sweat the Small Stuff: And It's All Small Stuff*[i]. I received this book as a gift many years ago. It's packed with simple, easy to follow advice. Dr. Carlson identifies 100 simple things we can do to help ourselves focus on the "here and now."

Each suggestion is followed by a brief description and some ideas on how to put it into practice. Here's a taste of the simple advice offered in the book;

- Remind yourself that when you die, your "in basket" won't be empty

- Don't interrupt others or finish their sentences for them

- Imagine that everyone is enlightened except you

- Become more patient

- Repeat this to yourself: "Life isn't an emergency"

- Experiment with your back burner

- Become a better listener

- Set aside some quiet time every day

- Smile at strangers, look into their eyes and say, "Hello"

- Breathe before you speak

- Understand the statement "Wherever you go, there you are"

- Become a less aggressive driver

- Remember you become what you practice most

- Stop blaming others

- The next time you find yourself in an argument, rather than defend your position see if you can see the other point of view first.

- Give up on the idea that more is better

- Live this day as if it were your last – it might be.

There are many other resources available on the topic of mindfulness. I encourage you to research and locate the ones that resonate with you. It doesn't have to be complicated or time consuming.

Set aside a few minutes each day to focus on this "inner work" – it is a worthwhile investment of time.

My Daily Mantra: A number of years ago my Mother gave me a bookmark that contained the following advice. I still have the bookmark but the advice I now recite by heart:

Just For Today ...

I will live through the next 12 hours and not try to tackle all of life's problems at once.

I will improve my mind. I will learn something useful. I will learn something that requires effort, thought and concentration.

I will be agreeable. I will look my best, speak in a well-modulated voice, and be courteous and considerate.

I will not find fault with friend, relative or colleague. I will not try to change or improve anyone but myself.

I will have a program. I may not follow it exactly, but I will have it. I will save myself from two enemies – hurry and indecision.

I will do a good turn and keep it a secret. If anyone finds out, it won't count.

I will do two things I don't want to do – just for the exercise.

I will believe in myself. I will give my best to the world and feel confident that the world will give its best to me.

— Author Unknown

Imagine being sufficiently disciplined to be able to practice all of the elements of this advice – all *of* the time.

I admit, I am a "work in progress." However, this advice has served me well in my work-life.

Finally, if you are like most of us, when we're reading an author's instructions or advice in a self-help book it all seems pretty straightforward.

Confusion sets in, though, when we try putting the information into practice.

Let me reassure you, and repeat advice you've read many times throughout this book: You've got this. Don't worry. You'll figure it out. You are exactly where you were meant to be.

Creating Your Career / Denise O'Brien

Manor House
905-648-4797
www.manor-house-publishing.com

www.ingramcontent.com/pod-product-compliance
Lightning Source LLC
LaVergne TN
LVHW011933070526
838202LV00054B/4627